TEXAS, MY TEXAS

TEXAS, MY TEXAS

MUSINGS OF
THE RAMBLING BOY

LONN TAYLOR

with a foreword by
Bryan Woollcy

TCU Press
Fort Worth, Texas

Library of Congress Cataloging-in-Publication Data
Taylor, Lonn, 1940-
Texas, my Texas : musings of the rambling boy / by Lonn Taylor.
p. cm.
ISBN 978-0-87565-434-8 (paper : alk. paper)
1. Texas–Social life and customs. 2. Texas–Description and travel. 3. Texas–
History. 4. Texas–History, Local. 5. Taylor, Lonn, 1940—Childhood and
youth. 6. Taylor, Lonn, 1940—Family. 7. Fort Davis (Tex.)–Social life and customs. 8. Fort Davis (Tex.)–History. 9. Fort Davis (Tex.)–Biography. I. Title.
F386.5.T39 2012
976.4–dc23
2011019637

TCU Press
P. O. Box 298300
Fort Worth, Texas 76129
817.257.7822
http://www.prs.tcu.edu
To order books:1.800.826.8911

designed & illustrated by
Barbara Mathews Whitehead

❖

For James Bratcher
of Bulverde
Scholar, Critic, Friend

CONTENTS

FOREWORD

I GREW UP in the preelectronic
age in Fort Davis, Texas, a tiny
village isolated from the greater world beyond the mountains and
desert that surrounded us. During my growing up, in the 1940s
and '50s, we had automobiles and telephones and electric lights
and indoor plumbing. During the day, we would listen to one
radio station, KVLF in Alpine, twenty-six miles away. (The VLF
stood for Voice of the Last Frontier.) At night we could tune in to
the clear-channel stations in Dallas, San Antonio, New Orleans,
and other big cities. We listened to Fibber Magee and Molly, Jack
Benny, Doctor IQ, and orchestras playing dance music in swanky
hotel nightclubs far away. Sometimes we would drive to Marfa or
Alpine and see a picture show. So we weren't deprived, even
though we had no video screens at which to stare, not even TV.

We also had stories. Everybody in Fort Davis, it seemed, had
stories to tell. Some of them were fiction, some fact, and some
were something in between. My grandmother, Clora Gibson, an
elementary school teacher who loved to read to her pupils and to
us, was as good a storyteller as Mark Twain. To this day, her telling
of "The Golden Arm" is scarier than any horror movie I've ever
seen. And great-uncles and great-aunts who came to visit would sit
on the porch and, to the rhythm of their rocking chairs, exchange
tales of long-dead ancestors, youthful loves, funny accidents, and
tragic deaths, remembered and passed down from their parents
and grandparents and from their own earlier lives. These stories
weren't fiction. They were family history and folklore. They taught
us about ourselves.

In the town outside our house there were stories about soldiers
who had served at the Old Fort, of cowboys and ranchers, of out-

laws and Rangers, and little rains and big droughts. A half-hour wait for a haircut at George Williams's barbershop, listening to the older customers swapping yarns, was an education and an entertainment.

Nearly all of that is gone now. Families are scattered across the planet. Grandmothers, parents, and children spend little time together. Uncles and aunts don't come to visit. They're staring into video screens like everybody else. No stories are told. No family or community history or folklore is passed on. Our roots are cut. And as a Fort Worth gentleman said to me years ago, "Without roots, we're nothing."

So let's be grateful to Lonn Taylor and his kind—people who still love digging into what someone has called "microhistory," into things that happen to people who aren't famous or powerful, and who pass their findings along to us.

Lonn does it in his column "The Rambling Boy," which appears in Marfa's excellent weekly newspaper, the *Big Bend Sentinel.* I subscribe to that paper, and I've been a fan of Lonn's work since the column first appeared in another Big Bend newspaper, now defunct. Lonn, a professional historian and former curator at the Smithsonian Institution, is also a fine writer and, most importantly, a storyteller in the grand Texas tradition. I've met him only once, but I consider him a friend. I'm glad he now lives in Fort Davis, the home of my soul, and is saving so much about the town and the Big Bend that otherwise might be lost.

This collection of some of his work is a treasure. I hope other volumes someday might follow.

Bryan Woolley
Dallas, Texas
March 2010

INTRODUCTION

I CONSIDER MYSELF a Texan, even though I was born else-where. My father was born in McKinney and grew up in Fort Worth. My mother was from Jacksboro. My father's career as a highway engineer for the United States Bureau of Public Roads took my parents away from Texas in the 1930s, first to South Carolina, where I was born, and then to Washington, DC, and finally to the Philippine Islands before they moved back to Fort Worth when I was sixteen. But three of my four great-grandfathers came to Texas before the Civil War and the fourth, a disgruntled ex-Confederate cavalryman, brought his family here from Louisiana shortly after the end of the war. In fact, one of my great-great grandfathers received a land grant in Fannin County from the Republic of Texas for being here before March 2, 1836, so I qualify for membership in the Sons of the Republic of Texas. I think my Texan credentials are as sound as Sam Houston's or Davy Crockett's or William Barrett Travis's, all of whom were born in other states.

My grandmother Taylor, the daughter of the Confederate cav-alryman, lived with us when I was a child, and her stories about her childhood on a series of rented Central Texas cotton farms kept my consciousness of my Texan inheritance alive while I was growing up away from Texas. When we moved to Fort Worth in 1956, the Texas past she talked about so much suddenly came into focus for me, and surrounded by the scenes of my father's boy-hood, I felt that I had come home.

I have always wanted to write about Texas. When I was seven my grandmother gave me a copy of J. Frank Dobie's *Legends of Texas*, the volume he edited for the Texas Folklore Society in 1924.

I devoured that book. It validated in print all my grandmother's stories. In fact, some of the tales in it were about people that my grandmother had known and that I had heard her talk about. Dobie's uncle, Jim Dobie, courted her little sister when her family lived at Lagarto, in Jim Wells County, and Judge W. P. McLean of Fort Worth, who hunted for Moro's gold, was a family friend. I realized for the first time that books could be about real events and people, and I decided then that someday I would be a writer and write those kinds of books.

During my career as a museum curator I wrote several books, but they were largely about objects rather than people. When I retired from the Smithsonian Institution in 2002, I moved back to Texas, and my wife and I built a house in Fort Davis. Kay Burnett, the widow of legendary West Texas lawyer Warren Burnett, was starting a weekly newspaper, the *Desert-Mountain Times*, in nearby Alpine. She asked me if I would write a column for it, saying that I could write about anything that I wanted. I have always admired George Dolan, who wrote a column called "This is West Texas" for the *Fort Worth Star-Telegram* in the 1960s, and Houston columnist Leon Hale, thinking that they had the best of all possible jobs, driving around the state talking to people and getting paid for it, so I said yes. But having just retired I did not want to tie myself to a weekly deadline, and so I stipulated that I would do one column every two weeks. I then sat down and wrote two columns and sent them in, thinking that my work for the month was done. Kay ran one column one week and one the next, and I became a weekly columnist.

I called my column "The Rambling Boy," after Tom Paxton's song, explaining to my readers that I would ramble around the Big Bend talking to people but that I would also ramble across Texas history for my subject matter. When the *Desert-Mountain Times* ceased publication, the column was picked up by Marfa's *Big Bend Sentinel*, which is still publishing it. Most of the pieces in this book first appeared in the *Big Bend Sentinel* and I am grateful to that paper's publisher, Robert Halpern, for his permission to republish them, as well as to Kay Burnett for her initial encouragement. I am also grateful to Al and Darlyne Lowman for making it possible for Barbara Whitehead to design and illustrate this book.

I have divided these essays into two major sections, one about Texas's past and one about present-day Texas, with an intervening section about some of the people who brought the past into the present for me. I have always found it difficult to separate the past from the present. The two seem to me to be bound together by stories, by old buildings, by the memories of old men and women. My grandmother Taylor was born in 1877; she carried her past into my childhood. My mother, who was born in 1902 and lived halfway though the last decade of the twentieth century, knew a woman, Bianca Babb, who had been stolen by Comanches as a child. Now that I have turned seventy I am increasingly aware of how much the 1950s and 1960s are still part of me. As William Faulkner famously wrote, "The past is not dead. In fact, it's not even past."

I am convinced that the history of Texas is a far more complex story than the cardboard cut-out narrative about the Alamo and Goliad that most Texans learned in their seventh-grade Texas history classes. In the essays about Texas's past I have tried to illustrate that complexity by avoiding the well-worn stories and concentrating instead on some of the people and incidents that the textbooks have passed by. In writing about present-day Texas, I freely admit that I have ignored the state's metropolises and written mostly about places where the past protrudes into the present and about people who are anachronisms. I live in a town of 1,160 people, with no traffic lights, where children say "ma'am" and "sir," and store clerks have time to gossip with their customers, and I like it. Towns like mine, and the people who live in them, provide a healthy counterbalance to the homogeneity, congestion, and heartlessness of modern urban life. John Graves once wrote about his rural neighbors in the countryside around Glen Rose that "there was a narrower choice of things for them to be . . . but they tended to make up for it by being what they were far more emphatically than most people these days are anything." I think that is a good thing and I take pleasure in recording it.

When I worked for the Texas State Historical Association at The University of Texas in the late 1960s, I walked daily past a framed placard in the old Barker Texas History Library. It contained a quotation from university librarian Ernest Winkler that read: "Texas history cannot be written without a sense of irony and a sense of humor." I have tried to follow that maxim in these essays.

I. TEXAS PAST

✤ 1 ✤

FORT DAVIS:
PLAZA OR SQUARE?

EVEN THOUGH it has a population of only 1,160 people, Fort
Davis can be a difficult town for strangers to find their way around
in. This was brought home to me one day when a houseguest managed to get lost walking from our house to the courthouse, which
is only four blocks away and whose clock tower is clearly visible
from our back porch. The problem, as our embarrassed guest
explained, is that several of our downtown streets intersect each
other at forty-five degree angles, and a careless turn can put a
pedestrian several blocks off course. These angles result from the
fact that Fort Davis was originally laid out on two separate but
adjoining grids. Those grids open a window into the two cultures
that shaped our town's and the Big Bend's history.

The two grids are the result of competition between Fort
Davis's two leading businessmen in the years just after the Civil
War, but they also reflect two competing ideas about urban land-
scape, one Catholic and Hispanic and one Protestant and Anglo-
American.

Daniel Murphy was an Irishman, born in County Cork, who
immigrated to the United States in his teens, served in the army
during the Mexican War, and ended up in San Antonio, where in
1852 he married Susan Hennesy, a native of County Antrim in
Ireland. When the young couple arrived in Fort Davis in 1855,
there was nothing here but the fort, which had been established
the year before, and the San Antonio-El Paso road, which the fort
was built to protect. Murphy took up land across the road from the
fort, where the Dirks-Anderson Elementary School is now, and

built an adobe hotel, saloon, and mercantile store. His customers were travelers on the El Paso road and soldiers at the fort. He prospered, and by 1860, at the age of thirty, he was the second-wealthiest man in Fort Davis, with real and personal property valued at $11,500.

The Murphys retreated to San Antonio during the Civil War, and Susan Murphy died there, leaving a son and five young daughters. Daniel Murphy married Susan's widowed sister, acquiring five more children, including four stepdaughters. The combined families returned to Fort Davis in 1868 and Murphy reopened his businesses. The Murphy home became the social center of the fort and four of the Murphy daughters married army officers.

The Murphys were devout Catholics, and in the 1870s, as the town of Fort Davis started to grow, Daniel Murphy donated the land due east of his home and store for a Catholic church and school. At about the same time he laid out a residential subdivision stretching five blocks southwest from his store, with the main street, now Davis Street, paralleling the El Paso road. He must have envisioned Fort Davis developing as a typical Hispanic town, like San Antonio or Presidio del Norte or the towns he had seen in Mexico, with the Catholic Church and the principal businesses fronting on a plaza. When that happened, Murphy's store and saloon would be on the plaza, across from the church, and the lots that he had laid out would increase in value due to their proximity to the plaza.

But things did not work out that way. Murphy's business rival in Fort Davis was Whitaker Keesey, a Yankee from Ohio who came to Fort Davis after the Civil War as a civilian employee of the army. Keesey also realized that the town was growing, and in 1874 he and his bother Otis homesteaded an eighty-acre tract of land a mile south of the fort, more or less in the middle of nowhere, and built a store on it. A year later the Texas legislature created Presidio County, which included Fort Davis, and Keesey immediately donated the block of land due west of his store for the county courthouse. Keesey knew that in Ohio courthouse squares, not churches, were the centers of towns, and he gambled that Fort Davis would develop in the same way, although he hedged his bet by donating another lot just south of the courthouse to the Methodist Church. Keesey's gamble paid off and he became an extremely wealthy man. His store prospered and became the largest mercantile enterprise between San Antonio and El Paso. He expanded the building several times after the courthouse was built across the street, and today the large rock structure he built in 1906 serves as the Jeff Davis County Public Library. You can still see his name, W. Keesey, carved in stone over the front door.

Whitaker Keesey had a friend, William Lempert, who came to Fort Davis at about the same time as Keesey and worked as a civilian clerk at the fort. Lempert was the stepson of an Eighth Infantry officer who had been stationed at the fort in the 1850s and he knew a good thing when he saw one. He acquired 160 acres adjoining Keesey's land north of the courthouse by the simple expedient of marrying Paula Ponce de Leon Robinson, the widow of the original grantee, in 1874. He built the Lempert Hotel, now the Veranda Bed and Breakfast, on his land in 1883 to accommodate citizens attending court, and then laid out a subdivision north and west of the hotel, now called the Home Addition. The Home Addition's main streets ran due north and south, parallel to the lines of Lempert's and Keesey's land grants. They intersected those of the Murphy Addition at forty-five degree angles, producing the confusion that caused our houseguest to get lost a hundred and twenty years later.

Whitaker Keesey sold his store in 1908 to a consortium of ranchers who formed the Union Trading Company, and today old-timers refer to the building as "the Union." In 1911, the Union Trading Company built the Limpia Hotel on a lot just northwest of the Union, and in 1913, the same group of ranchers incorporated the Fort Davis State Bank and built a handsome rock building to house it southwest of the Union. Those two buildings, along

with the new courthouse built in 1910 and Keesey's Union building, produced a courthouse square as fine as any in Ohio.
Murphy's plaza never materialized, and tourists still get confused
trying to navigate between the courthouse and the fort, and possi-
bly between the two cultures that coexist here.

November 12, 2009

LOS CIBOLEROS
IN THE PANHANDLE

MOST TWENTY-FIRST century
Texans would probably be
surprised to learn that long before the Texas Panhandle was
famous for cattle and oil, in fact long before the boundaries were
drawn that made it the Panhandle, it was Far Eastern New Mexico
to the Hispanic settlers along the upper Rio Grande. In the early
1700s, men and women from Taos, Santa Cruz, Chimayo, and
other villages north of Santa Fe began to venture out onto the eastern plains each year to hunt buffalo and occasionally trade with
the Comanches who lived there. They were known as *los
ciboleros*—the buffalo-ers—and the more sedentary settlers to the
south thought they were absolute wild men. A ballad from the
early 1800s describes "the people from Chimayo with their braided
hair, who have left their looms . . ."

The *ciboleros* wore wide-bottomed knee-length leather pants,
high leather boots, leather jackets, and peaked leather caps with
feathers in them—there is a painting of one on a door from Santa
Cruz at the Museum of International Folk Art in Santa Fe—and
they carried eight-foot-long lances with foot-long iron tips as well
as bows and arrows. Every fall, after the crops were harvested and
when the buffalo were fat and the wool was thick on their hides,
the *ciboleros* went out onto the plains on horseback, accompanied
by ox-drawn carts which carried the dried meat and hides back to
the settlements.

A single party of *ciboleros* might include 150 men and women,
500 horses and pack mules, and 50 carts. Some of the nineteenth-

century *ciboleros* who survived into the 1930s told Federal Writers' Project interviewer Lorin Brown how the hunt worked. The men elected a leader, a *comandante*, who was in absolute charge of the group. When they spotted a herd of buffalo, the *comandante* called all the men together and had them recite the Apostles' Creed. Then he gave the order to charge by shouting "Ave Maria Purisima!" and the hunters fanned out across the prairie, with the fastest horses and the most skilled hunters on the flanks. When the killing was over, the women helped to skin the buffalo and cut up and dry the meat. They frequently got as far as the Canadian River in the Panhandle and brought back an astonishing amount of meat and hides; an 1812 report estimated that the *ciboleros* killed 10,000 to 12,000 buffalo each year.

Sometimes the *ciboleros* brought back more than meat and hides. One of the more colorful characters around Santa Cruz in the nineteenth century was a man called *El Guero* Mestas, who died in his eighties about 1890. *El Guero* had blond hair and blue eyes—thus his nickname—and he had been brought to Santa Cruz as an infant by some *ciboleros* who had traded buffalo meat for him with a band of Comanches they had met in the breaks of the Canadian River. The Comanches had killed his parents and were taking him back to adopt into their tribe. Instead, he was adopted by a family named Mestas and grew up to be a prosperous farmer and prominent man in Santa Cruz, famous for his poetry, his practical jokes, and his piercing blue eyes.

The *ciboleros* didn't always get what they went after. Vicente Romero of Cordova told Lorin Brown about a trip he made to the Texas plains. He and his companions met up with a group of Comanches and camped with them to do some trading. The wife of one of the Indians turned out to be a young Mexican girl from San Antonio, Texas, who had been taken captive a few years before. She pleaded with Romero to rescue her, and Romero considered the sensation it would cause at home if he brought the beautiful captive back as a bride. But the *comandante* told him,

"No, it can't be done. Any effort to free her might destroy our whole party." When Romero's friend Anaclete Mascarenas continued to argue with the *comandante,* he was seized and bound until he promised to obey the leader's orders in everything. "So," Romero concluded, "the *pobrecita* stayed there with the Indians, perhaps for life. *Asi le toco* [thus it happened]."

As the buffalo herds diminished, the *ciboleros* turned to trading with the Comanches, taking salt, tobacco, Navajo blankets, strips of iron, dried fruit, and sacks of a hard bread called *pan de Comanche* out on the Texas plains and coming back with horses, stolen cattle, and, sometimes, captives like *El Guero* Mestas. Santa Fe trader Josiah Gregg met a group of these traders on the plains in the 1820s and claimed that they spent so much time with the Comanches that they pointed at objects with their chins, like Indians, instead of with their fingers. By the 1850s and '60s *comancheros,* as these traders were called, were meeting with Comanches at springs and creeks all over the Panhandle, and some people were unkind enough to say that they even accompanied their trading partners on raids to ranches in the Cross Timbers and the Hill Country so they could pick out the cattle they wanted.

In 1876 a former *comanchero* from Mora, Casimero Romero, decided to settle permanently in the Panhandle, and he brought his family, 100 servants, and 5,500 sheep to Atascosa Creek in Oldham County, where he built a big adobe house, dug irrigation ditches, and gathered several other families from Mora and Las Vegas around him. He and his neighbors prospered as New Mexican sheep ranchers in Texas for a few years, but then cattlemen began to crowd them out and they pulled back across the plains to New Mexico and left the Panhandle to the cattlemen, who are still there. But the next time you drive to Lubbock, think not about ranchers and wildcatters, but about the *ciboleros* from Chimayo with their braided hair and leather jackets and lances.

September 14, 2006

✛ 3 ✛

THE PAYNES,
BLACK SEMINOLE COWBOYS

NOT LONG AGO I was talking with Nora Payne Geron, an Alpine native who now lives in Pecos. She was telling me a little about her father's family, who, like many people in the Big Bend, came to Texas from Mexico in the early years of the twentieth century. Geron grew up on a ranch outside of Alpine and spoke Spanish as a child. "In fact," she told me, "I didn't know there was any other language until I started school." But there was something different about Geron's family. Her father, Rocky Payne, was descended from the Black Seminoles.

The Black Seminoles are a people with a proud and unusual heritage. Their eighteenth-century ancestors were black slaves who escaped from plantations in South Carolina and found refuge among the Seminole villages of Spanish Florida. When the United States acquired Florida and deported the Seminoles to Oklahoma, the Black Seminoles, as they came to be called, went with them. But in the 1840s, fearful of being sold back into slavery, a group of Black Seminole families left Oklahoma and made their way into northern Mexico. The Mexican government gave them a land grant near Musquiz in return for military service against the Apaches and Comanches, and many of the men married local women. In 1870, when the US Army made them the same offer, some crossed the Rio Grande into Texas. The army's offer of land evaporated, but two generations of Black Seminoles served valiantly as members of a unit called the Negro Seminole Indian Scouts, stationed at Fort Clark, near Brackettville.

Although they never received their promised land grant, the army allowed them to build cabins for their families on the Fort Clark reservation. Then, when the unit was dissolved in 1914, they were expelled from Fort Clark, their cabins were razed, and they were told to fend for themselves. Some scattered over West Texas, the men often taking jobs as cowboys.

Two who came to the Big Bend were Geron's grandfather and great-uncle, Monroe and John Payne, both of whom had been born at Fort Clark in the 1870s, the children of Scout Nato Mariscal and his wife, Dolly Payne. The Paynes were an important family among the Black Seminole, probably related in some way to the Florida Seminole chief known as King Payne, and Nato Mariscal's children took the name Payne. When Mariscal took his discharge from the scouts, he took his family back to the Black Seminole settlement in Mexico, and his sons grew up there and married local women. Monroe Payne came to Brewster County in 1904 and his brother John came in 1914, after having served for a while in one of the revolutionary armies in Mexico. Both became legendary cowboys, as did their sons. Monroe Payne was foreman of the Lou Butrill Ranch in the Rosillos Mountains for several years. He eventually acquired a considerable amount of property and moved to Marathon, where he ran a freight business and engaged in a number of other business enterprises. Even though he was considered "colored" by his neighbors, he is remembered as a man of great personal dignity who deferred to no one. He once pistol-whipped a white cowboy who insulted him and suffered none of the consequences that would normally have devolved on a black man in Texas at that time. He died in 1952.

Monroe Payne's brother, John, worked for several South Brewster County ranchers after he came across the river and eventually became foreman of the legendary Combs Ranch near Marathon, a job he held for the rest of his life. His son, Blas Payne, also worked for the Combses and succeeded his father as foreman. He is remembered by many who worked with him as the best cowboy they ever saw, a man who had an instinctive way with horses. Monroe Payne's son, Rocky, Nora Geron's father, was also widely known for his ability with horses. He worked for the Gage Ranch and the 06, and eventually became foreman of the Que Decie outside of Alpine. He was also known for his sense of humor. Ted Gray of Alpine tells a good story on him. They were hunting wild cattle together on the 06, and Gray saw a young bull emerge from a thicket dragging a rope. When he asked whose rope it was, Rocky Payne said, "It's his'n. I gave it to him over in that brush thicket. He can keep it now."

There have been many African American cowboys in the West, but few have been bearers of such a complex heritage as the Paynes, and few have risen to such positions of responsibility in the ranching world.

September 15, 2005

✦ 4 ✦

"AN UNFORTUNATE ADMIXTURE OF AFRICAN BLOOD"

IRECENTLY FOUND myself thinking about Samuel McCulloch. Samuel McCulloch was the first man wounded in the Texas Revolution. He was in the company of volunteers that stormed the Mexican fort at Goliad in the pre-dawn darkness of October 9, 1835, and he got a musket ball in the shoulder that troubled him the rest of his life.

As a result, he received a special bounty grant of one league of land—4,400 acres—from the Republic of Texas under a law that rewarded wounded veterans of the Revolution. As a settler who came to Texas before March 2, 1836, he was also entitled to a head-right grant of an additional 4,600 acres, or a total of 9,000 acres. But McCulloch had a problem. He was part black. As he put it in one of the petitions he filed with the Texas legislature in his repeated attempts to get his land, he "had an unfortunate admixture of African blood." Because of this, even though he had fought for Texas's freedom, he was not permitted to own land in or even reside in the Republic of Texas without the special permission of the Republic's Congress.

I think about Samuel McCulloch every once in a while because his story exemplifies the complexity and irony and ultimate tragedy of nineteenth century (and maybe some twenty-first century) Texans' attitude about race.

McCulloch came to Texas when it was still part of Mexico with his white father, three sisters, and two African American women named Peggy and Rose, one of whom was probably his mother and the other, her sister. McCulloch's father later said in a petition that he brought the women to Mexican Texas "desiring that they should be free." Mexican law, while permitting slavery in Texas, did not prohibit intermarriage between the races and made no distinction between free African Americans and other Mexican citizens. A number of interracial couples and free blacks came to Texas before 1836 to take advantage of these conditions.

When Texas became an independent republic in 1836, the McCulloch family and others like them found themselves back in the Old South. The new republic's constitution prohibited interracial marriage, deprived free blacks of citizenship, and forbade them to reside in Texas without the permission of Congress. McCulloch, who married a white woman in 1837 and farmed on his father's land in Jackson County, applied for the land to which he was entitled in 1838. He was given a certificate for his bounty land but he was denied both his citizenship and his head-right land because he was black.

In 1840, Samuel McCulloch and his family faced another challenge. On February 5 of that year the Texas Congress passed an act requiring all free blacks living within the republic to leave Texas within two years or to sell themselves into slavery. McCulloch submitted a petition signed by a large number of his neighbors asking that he, his three sisters, and a relative named Uldy be exempted from this act. In November 1840 Congress passed a relief bill permitting the McCullochs to remain unhampered in Texas.

McCulloch continued to petition and lobby for his head-right land and his citizenship. Finally in 1858, after a tremendous effort on his part, the Seventh Legislature passed an act granting him his head-right certificate. He located his land in Bexar County, near the little town of Von Ormy, and moved his family there. His marriage was never considered legal.

Forty years ago I wrote an article about Samuel McCulloch for the supplement to *The Handbook of Texas*. In order to check his death date, I drove out to the McCulloch family cemetery at Von Ormy. I found his tombstone and his death date, November 1, 1893, and then I noticed his son's tombstone. Its inscription said: "William R. McCulloch, Colonel, Confederate States Army." While I was pondering this, a man drove up in a pickup and asked what I was looking for. When I explained, he told me that there were still McCullochs living nearby and directed me to their house. I spent the rest of the afternoon with them, drinking iced tea on their porch. They were proud of their ancestor's participation in the Revolution and if they were aware of his African American ancestry, they did not mention it.

Later that evening, in a local café, I was talking to an old rancher sitting on the stool next to me and I told him where I had spent the afternoon. "Oh, yeah," he said, "the McCullochs. Nice people. You know, they're supposed to be part n   ."

I still don't know exactly what all this means. It just makes me sad.

June 2, 2005

✤ 5 ✤

HEAT, DUST, AND BOREDOM

SINCE EVERYONE in Fort Davis volunteers for something, I decided shortly after we moved here to put my training as a historian to good use and volunteer at the fort, which is a National Park Service Historic Site.

The historian there, Mary Williams, put me to work indexing the microfilmed documents in the library. I worked on the daily records of the fort for the 1880s, microfilmed from the originals in the Library of Congress. If you were ever in the armed forces, you know that Napoleon was wrong when he said that an army marches on its stomach. An army marches on paper—reams of it. Even in the nineteenth century no soldier could move half a mile, nor could the ordinary business of a military post be carried on, without some sort of form or document being prepared in triplicate. There is nothing like reading hundreds of original documents to get the flavor of a time and place.

The flavor of Fort Davis in the 1880s was hot, dusty, and suffused with boredom. I learned a lot about how the army worked in those days. I learned that the soldiers at Fort Davis didn't worry about fighting Indians. They worried about keeping track of government property. Every third document that I read was a request for a board of survey—a committee of three officers—to be appointed in order to "investigate and fix responsibility for" the loss of a saddle blanket, or damage to a firearm, or a discrepancy between an invoice for peas and the number of sacks delivered. Hours and hours of military time was spent literally counting beans, and the person responsible for the missing beans had their cost deducted from his pay.

A private back then earned thirteen dollars a month. Privates could supplement their pay by doing extra duty as blacksmiths, tailors, carpenters, teamsters, stonemasons, hospital stewards, or laborers in the quartermaster department. Each month the company commanders were required to turn in a list of "mechanics and clerks" in their companies in order to identify men who might qualify for these jobs. Skilled men got an additional thirty-five cents a day for extra duty; laborers were paid twenty cents extra a day. The papers at the fort record weekly assignments to and relief from extra duty.

Sometimes the personality of a soldier can be glimpsed behind the formal military language. In 1887 a private was relieved of extra duty as a teamster "due to the constant surveillance to which his intemperate habits require him to be subjected." A year earlier, an officer vetoed an extra duty assignment by noting on the document that the man "was entirely worthless as a soldier and appears to be incapable of reformation."

Extra duty not only added to a private's income, it helped to relieve boredom, which was a big factor in life at the fort in the 1880s. In the previous decade, bands of Apaches occasionally raided remote ranches and held up stagecoaches in the Big Bend, keeping the soldiers on their toes. But the Victorio Campaign of 1881 marked the end of Indian fighting here, and for the next ten years, until the post was closed in 1891, the army pretty much twiddled its thumbs.

The depth of the boredom is revealed in a series of documents at the fort dated in September of 1889. The fort had a steam-powered ice machine, which was fired with pine logs cut on the slopes of Mount Livermore at a place called The Pinery. In early September 1889, someone decided that someone else was stealing wood from the fort's woodpile and charging it up to the ice machine. The case assumed the dimensions of Captain Queeg's missing strawberry ice cream. An order came down from the post commander, Lt. Col. Melville A. Cochran, that a board of review should be formed to determine exactly how much wood the ice machine burned each day. For two weeks, a captain and two lieutenants met every day to consider the ice machine. They ran it from six thirty in the morning until nine at night for three days straight. They weighed and measured the wood that went into its engine and the cans of ice that came out of it. They interviewed the men who loaded the wood wagon, the man who drove it, the sergeant who supervised them, and the hospital steward who ran the machine.

They tabulated the usage of wood all over the fort, which came to seventy-seven cords for the month of August—no wonder the mountains around Fort Davis are bare of timber. At the end of September, they sat down and drafted a forty-page handwritten report that concluded that some unknown person was stealing wood from the woodpile and charging it to the ice machine.

The Fourth of July 1890 was definitely not a boring day at the fort. A handbill advertising the activities that day is preserved in the fort's archives. There was a morning baseball game between the Twenty-Third Infantry and the Old Nine, followed by free coffee, tea, and sandwiches and an afternoon of athletic events, including foot races, broad jumps, a sack race, a wheelbarrow race, a greased pig race, and a twenty-four-man tug-of-war, "soldiers against civilians." There was also a 400-yard horse race, with "Mr. Dan Knight's fast horse ruled out." The prize was twenty-five dollars, a lot of money in 1890.

But the handbill tells only part of the story. That evening, after the races were over and the soldiers had headed for the bars just outside the fort's perimeter, a tremendous thunderstorm broke. A microfilmed document in the fort's archives reveals what happened next. Lieutenant S. A. Dyer wrote to the post commander the next day, explaining that at the height of the storm he was running across the parade ground to the post chapel and, in a flash of lightning, he saw the post adjutant, Lieutenant Edwards, running towards him. He thought that, as they passed each other, Edwards shouted at him to have the bugle call "Assembly" sounded, so when Dyer reached the chapel and found a musician there, he ordered the man to step outside and blow the call.

Edwards endorsed Dyer's report, saying that Dyer had misunderstood him, but the immediate result was that three hundred inebriated soldiers came stumbling out of their barracks or running from the cantinas to form ranks on the parade ground in the driving rain, and no one knew why they were there. None of them ever forgot that Fourth of July.

December 18, 2003

✤ 6 ✤

THE EPIC OF HENRY O. FLIPPER

ONE OF THE PLEASURES of living in far West Texas is the series of readings given by the Lannan Foundation's resident writers at the Marfa Book Company on Saturday nights. Several weeks ago the reader was the poet Marilyn Nelson. Nelson is an African American woman in her early sixties whose totally unlined face radiates an inner joy when she reads; listening to her is an extraordinary experience. She has written several long narrative poems on themes from African American history, including "Carver," based on incidents in the life of George Washington Carver.

At the reception following the reading, Nelson expressed interest in an incident that happened in Fort Davis in 1881, saying that it would be a good subject for a narrative poem. She was referring, of course, to the court martial and dismissal from the army of Lt. Henry O. Flipper, who in 1877 became the first African American graduate of West Point and who, at the time of his trial, was the only black officer in the US Army. Flipper's career would indeed be a good subject for a poem, since it combines pride, ambition, tragedy, human failure, and resilience: the stuff that epic poetry is made of. Flipper's ordeal is often presented as a story of pure racism, a conspiracy of white officers to get rid of a black officer, and indeed this was the way that Flipper told the story in his memoirs, written in 1916, and in the petitions for reinstatement that he sent to Congress. But the facts are much more complicated than that.

Although Flipper was ostracized because of his race by his fellow cadets at West Point, he earned the respect and friendship of most of the officers he served with during his four years of active duty with the Tenth Cavalry. His regimental commander, Col. Benjamin Grierson, said that during that short time he had "steadily won his way by sterling worth and ability, by manly and soldierly bearing, to the confidence and esteem of all with whom he has served or come in contact with." When his troubles started he was on his way to a promising army career.

Flipper's downfall may have been partially due to the army's complex financial system, which assigned to officers who had no training in fiscal management the responsibility for handling large sums of money. When Flipper was posted to Fort Davis in 1880 he was made Acting Commissary of Subsistence for the fort, which meant that he was responsible for collecting money for groceries sold from the post commissary to officers and enlisted men, and for transmitting that money monthly to the Department of Texas headquarters in San Antonio. For some reason that has never been satisfactorily explained, Flipper kept the cash, currency, and checks that he collected in a trunk in his quarters rather than in the safe at the commissary. In July 1881, he discovered that there was less money in the trunk than there should have been—he was nearly $2,400 short. Part of the discrepancy was his own commissary bill of $1,100, but the rest had probably been pilfered by his servant or taken by one of the many civilian visitors who frequented his quarters. Flipper then did two things that he never should have done. He made out a false report for the post commander, Col. William Shafter, to sign, saying that the total due was in hand and would be forwarded to San Antonio, and he wrote a check on a non-existent account in a San Antonio bank to cover some of the missing funds. Shafter signed the report and ordered Flipper to forward the funds to San Antonio, and Flipper assured Shafter he would do so. Instead, he sat on the funds, hoping he could find some way to make up the rest of the missing money, and continued to give Shafter weekly reports to sign saying that the funds were in transit. Eventually, a telegram from San Antonio informed

Shafter that the funds had not arrived, and Flipper dug himself a deeper hole by assuring Shafter that he had sent them in. Shafter at first thought that there had been a mail robbery, but when he learned that none had taken place, he concluded that Flipper had appropriated the money for his own use and had him arrested. A court martial was convened, and Flipper was charged with two separate offenses: embezzlement and conduct unbecoming an officer and a gentleman. After a month of deliberation, the court exonerated Flipper of the first charge, because there was no evidence that he had appropriated the money for his own use, but convicted him on the second, because it was clear that he had prepared false reports, written a hot check, and lied to the post commander. The penalty specified in the Articles of War was automatic dismissal from the army. Flipper's army career came to an end when he was only twenty-six.

The intriguing thing about Flipper is that having stumbled once, he never stumbled again. He went on to have a productive civilian career as a mining engineer, a historian, and an expert on Spanish and Mexican land grants in the Southwest. He opened an engineering office in Nogales, Arizona, and in the 1890s he was retained as a special agent by the US Court of Private Land Claims. He befriended and gained the confidence of the most prominent land lawyers in the Southwest, including two future cabinet members, William Gibbs McAdoo and Albert B. Fall, both of whom employed him as a translator. He published the first English translation of Pedro de Castañeda's account of the 1539 Fray Marcos de Niza expedition into the Southwest, an expedition guided by a black man, the Moorish slave Estevanico. In the 1920s, he helped William F. Buckley Sr. establish his Pantepec Oil Company in Venezuela. He lost his investments and savings in the 1929 stock market crash and died penniless in 1940.

In later life Flipper became obsessed with his dismissal from the army and convinced himself that it was due to racial prejudice. In 1898, when he was in his forties, he submitted a petition to Congress for reinstatement in the army, and he continued to submit petitions until 1924. None of these petitions were successful. In 1976 an army board reopened his case and upgraded his dismissal to an honorable discharge, and in 1999 Flipper was granted a pardon by President Clinton. The tragedy is that had Flipper simply walked into Shafter's office that morning in 1881 and stated the facts, that he was short in his accounts and did not know what had happened to the money, he might have retired from the army as a colonel, full of age and honor. Surely his life has the makings of an epic poem.

February 26, 2009

✤ 7 ✤

CHARLIE SIRINGO AND THE PINKERTONS

THERE ARE HUNDREDS of books about cowboys—I've even written one myself—but the very first, and maybe the best, was written by a native Texan, Charles Angelo Siringo. He wrote it when he was only thirty, in 1885, but he started cowboying at the age of fifteen, so he had a lot of experiences to pack into it. Siringo called his book *A Texas Cowboy, or Fifteen Years on the Hurricane Deck of a Spanish Pony.* The subtitle was a sly allusion to the popularity of nautical memoirs at the time, particularly those of whalers. Siringo almost singlehandedly changed that. The publication of *A Texas Cowboy* marked the beginning of a shift of America's national hero from the sailor to the cowboy.

Siringo had a lot to write about. He was born in Matagorda, and he started out working for some of the legendary cattlemen of the Texas coast—W. B. Grimes and Abel Head "Shanghai" Pierce. In the mid-1870s he became a trail driver and took several herds up the Chisholm Trail to Kansas, where he got his chance to "whoop 'em up, Liza Jane," as he put it, in Wichita and Dodge City. On one of his trips to Dodge City he met two men who wanted to establish a ranch in the Panhandle, so he took a herd there and helped to locate the headquarters of the 187,000-acre LX Ranch in Potter County. He worked for the LX for a few years and had an encounter with Billy the Kid when the owners sent him to New Mexico to recover stolen cattle. When he was twenty-nine he married, quit cowboying, and settled down in Caldwell, Kansas, to run a tobacco shop and ice cream parlor and write his book. He probably thought that his adventures were over and looked forward to a long and prosperous life as a small-town merchant.

But his book catapulted him into a new career, one that most people who have read A *Texas Cowboy* have no idea about. He printed and distributed the book himself, and it was a tremendous success, so he decided to bring out a second edition through a Chicago publishing company, and he moved his family to Chicago so that he could oversee the printing. The Haymarket bombings took place shortly after he arrived, and Siringo impulsively joined the Pinkerton Detective Agency to help track down the anarchists who were allegedly responsible. In those pre-FBI days the Pinkerton Agency was the closest thing the country had to a national police agency. Even though it was privately owned, it had resources far beyond those available to local sheriffs or even big-city police chiefs. The Pinkerton Agency was Siringo's introduction to the modern urban world, which he quickly discovered ran on very different principles from the cattle business. He found he was expected to pad his expense accounts, falsify evidence, and overlook the criminal activities of some of his colleagues in the agency. Even though he stayed with the Pinkertons for twenty-two years and participated in some of their most famous cases, he never completely reconciled himself to their methods. He used his savings to buy a small ranch outside of Santa Fe, New Mexico, which he named Sunny Slope Ranch and to which he intended to retire.

He did retire there in 1907, and began writing his second book. It was a tell-all autobiography called *Pinkerton's Cowboy Detective, A True Story of 22 Years with Pinkerton's National Detective Agency*. When the Pinkerton Agency saw the prepublication posters advertising the book they went absolutely crazy. They managed to get the galley sheets from Siringo's Chicago publisher and had an injunction issued forbidding the book's publication on the grounds that it was libelous. In the ensuing negotiations,

Siringo agreed to drop the name "Pinkerton" from the title and to delete all references to the agency from the text, as well as to change the names of all the agents mentioned. The book was eventually published in 1912 under the title A *Cowboy Detective*, but the incident rankled with Siringo the rest of his life. He stewed about it for two years and then sat down and wrote a third book entitled *Two Evil Isms: Pinkertonism and Anarchism*. This time he pulled out all the stops. He accused the Pinkertons of bribing juries, corrupting public employees, fixing elections, kidnapping witnesses, and knowingly causing the execution of innocent men. Then to top it off he sent the manuscript to the Pinkerton Agency's New York office, with a request that they read it and notify him of any "objectionable features." It took the agency less than a New York minute to get an injunction against its publication, and when Siringo went ahead and printed it (with a cover that showed Uncle Sam entwined by two snakes, one labeled "Anarchism" and one labeled "Pinkertonism") they got a Chicago judge to issue a warrant for his arrest. Governor William McDonald of New Mexico, who was an old cowboy friend of Siringo's, refused to extradite him, and the Pinkertons were reduced to buying up all of the copies of the book they could find on newsstands and destroying them. The old Texas cowboy taught the Pinkertons a lesson: Don't mess with Texas.

In the late 1920s, Siringo moved to Hollywood, where he became one of a group of old-timers who hung around the film studios and advised actors like William S. Hart on proper Western behavior. He was part of a circle that included Charlie Russell, Eugene Manlove Rhodes, Will James, and the reformed outlaw Emmett Dalton. He even wrote another book, *Riata and Spurs*, which was published by a major publisher, Houghton Mifflin. But I can never drive past Siringo Road in Santa Fe, the road that led to Sunny Slope Ranch, without thinking of the way the Texas cowboy tweaked the nose of the Pinkertons.

August 24, 2006

✢ 8 ✢

NOAH SMITHWICK, BLACKSMITH
AND MEMOIRIST

A FEW WEEKS AGO, a friend of mine who teaches a Texas history course at TCU sent out an Internet request for suggestions for supplementary reading for his students. Most of his respondents suggested scholarly monographs that were in-depth explorations of subjects that were touched on lightly in the textbook, which is what most college course supplementary reading is, but for some reason I thought of a book I haven't picked up in years. Noah Smithwick's *Evolution of a State*, first published in 1900.

Smithwick was by no means a scholar. He was a blacksmith, and he subtitled his book *Recollections of Old Texas Days*. That is exactly what it is, a memoir of his life in Texas between 1827 and 1861. It was a fairly ordinary life. Smithwick was neither exceptionally brave nor exceptionally lucky, and if he could avoid trouble, he did. But he had two outstanding qualities: he had a gift for friendship, and he wrote with verve and gusto about the things that happened to him and his friends. He also had a sense of humor, and he had been polishing some of his stories for fifty or sixty years before he set them down. Here's a sample: the town ne'er-do-well was hanging around Smithwick's blacksmith shop in Burnett, staring into the white-hot forge. He remarked on how hot the forge must be. Smithwick said, "Oh, that's not half as hot as you'll have to stand when you go to hell, and that will last forever."

"That's all a lie," the man replied. "If hell is half as hot as that, a dead man wouldn't last a minute there."

Actually, Smithwick didn't exactly set these stories down, he dictated them to his daughter, because he was ninety years old and blind when he finally got around to writing about his life.

Smithwick came to Texas from Kentucky when he was nineteen and set up as a blacksmith in the capital of Austin's colony, San Felipe, which he describes as "twenty-five or perhaps thirty log cabins strung along the west bank of the Brazos," and he stayed there until 1831. His account of life at San Felipe during those years is absolutely the best in print. His descriptions of the characters who hung around the town and their entertainments are unvarnished, to say the least, and the Daughters of the Republic of Texas would probably not approve of them. San Felipe was largely a bachelor society, and a great deal of alcohol was consumed. People made their own fun. A popular form of entertainment was a dinner at which each guest was expected to offer a recitation or a song, and at which the flowing bowl circulated freely. One of Smithwick's friends was Judge Robert M. Williamson, known as "Three-Legged Willie" because his right leg was withered below the knee and he wore a peg leg strapped to his kneecap. Williamson was much in demand at these dinners because he could produce a one-man minstrel show, imitate a country school spelling bee, and parody revival sermons. Smithwick recounts that early one morning following such a dinner he heard a voice under his window calling, "O, Smithwick, here's a man with a broken leg." He went outside to find Williamson with his peg leg splintered, the result of a fall. He helped the judge into his shop, fired up his forge, and stapled the wooden leg back together with iron clamps.

Dances were another form of entertainment, especially when families with marriageable daughters began to arrive in the colony. As there was only one fiddler available, his instrument was often supplemented. Smithwick describes one dance at which the fiddle could scarcely be heard over the clomping boots, so the rhythm was picked out by a man hitting a plow clevis with a hammer, and another at which the fiddler was absent, so the music was supplied by the plow clevis and a second man scraping a cotton hoe with a clasp knife.

There was a certain group at San Felipe who thought themselves more refined than Smithwick and his friends, and they used to complain that society in Texas would improve when "the better sort" finally got there. Smithwick tells about meeting an old San Felipe friend, Walter White, on a street in Bastrop in the 1850s, thirty years after their San Felipe days. White had operated a store in San Felipe, and used to leave his goods piled up on the riverbank for days at a time, confident that no one would steal anything. As Smithwick and White walked along the street talking, they passed a store in front of which lay a pile of heavy millstones that were chained and padlocked to the store's porch. "Gad, Smithwick," White said, gesturing at the millstones, "the better sort must have finally got here!"

In summing up the population of that little community, Smithwick wrote, "Many hard things have been said or written of the early settlers of Texas, much of which is unfortunately only too true." Many of his companions were living under assumed names, having committed some crime in the United States. He quotes one of his friends as saying, "People were nearer on an equal footing socially in San Felipe than any place you ever saw; if one said to another, 'You ran away,' he could retort, 'So did you.'" But Smithwick clearly enjoyed the four years he spent there, and relished telling about them for the rest of his life.

July 29, 2006

✤ 9 ✤

TEDDY ROOSEVELT IN TEXAS

THE BAR of the Menger Hotel in San Antonio is a vaguely Gothic oak-paneled room that, for many years, was presided over by a dour coffee-colored man named Freeman. Freeman once bought me a cold Pearl and lent me five dollars when I stopped in on my way from Nuevo Laredo to Austin with nothing but a Texaco credit card and a dollar bill in my wallet. According to the hotel's publicity department, the bar is a replica of the bar in the House of Lords, fabricated in England in the 1870s and shipped to San Antonio to be assembled in the hotel. This claim proved to be impossible for me to verify on a trip to London because I was told that one had to be a member of the House of Lords to gain admission to their bar and that I clearly did not qualify. When I told Freeman about this, he said that he did not blame them and that sometimes he had doubts about letting me into his bar.

Another tale about the Menger Bar, also vigorously promoted by the hotel's management, is that it is where Teddy Roosevelt recruited volunteers for the Rough Riders, the volunteer cavalry regiment that Roosevelt took to Cuba in 1898. There might be a grain of truth in that claim, because the Rough Riders, officially known as the First Volunteer United States Cavalry, encamped at San Antonio's International Fair Grounds for three weeks in May 1898, and it took San Antonians a long time to recover from having a regiment of cowboys in their midst.

The idea of a cavalry regiment made up of hard-riding, crack shot western cowboys was first suggested to Roosevelt in the early 1880s by his friend Baron Hermann Speck von Sternburg, a German diplomat who was fascinated with Roosevelt's stories about his western hunting trips. In 1886, during a political crisis with Mexico, Roosevelt proposed the idea to Massachusetts Congressman Henry Cabot Lodge, but the crisis passed without a declaration of war. In April 1898, when the United States declared war on Spain, several western governors offered to raise volunteer cowboy regiments. Secretary of War Russell Alger, recalling Roosevelt's earlier proposal, asked Roosevelt to take charge of them. Roosevelt, aware of his own lack of military experience, suggested that his friend, regular army surgeon Col. Leonard Wood, be placed in command, and that he be second in command. Alger assented. But from the start Roosevelt's ebullient personality dominated the regiment, and the press dubbed them "Roosevelt's Rough Riders."

It was Roosevelt who thought of adding a contingent of Ivy League sportsmen to the group—polo players, big-game hunters, and yachtsmen. Recruiting started in late April 1898. The western volunteers were enrolled at Prescott, Arizona; Santa Fe, New Mexico; Guthrie, Oklahoma; and Muskogee, Indian Territory. The easterners signed up in Boston and Washington, DC. The regiment assembled in San Antonio the first week in May, with the various contingents arriving by train. They were a picturesque sight as they climbed down from their coaches at the fairground siding in cowboy dress, and San Antonians flocked to see them unload. The Arizonans brought along a mascot, a golden-yellow mountain lion named Josephine. Many of the Oklahomans were Choctaw, Cherokee, Chicasaw, and Creek Indians.

After they set up camp, the regiment's first order of business was to saddle-break the horses that the army had purchased for them at thirty dollars a head. This was done on a volunteer basis, with the bronco-busters being excused from drill. Roosevelt later wrote, "We had an abundance of men who were utterly unmoved by any antic a horse might commit." Several thousand San Antonians showed up to watch the fun, as word had gone around town that it would be better than Buffalo Bill's Wild West (in fact, after they came back from Cuba, a dozen Rough Riders organized a special riding act for Buffalo Bill). The first trainload of easterners arrived in the middle of the horse-breaking, and they were greeted with whoops and cheers by the cowboys, who had already dubbed the passengers the "Fifth Avenue Dudes." One of them, a man wearing a business suit and a derby hat, walked over to the horse lines, pointed to a particularly unsavory-looking animal, and asked if he could have a try. He swung into the saddle as the westerners exchanged knowing smirks, waiting for the volcanic explosion that they were sure was about to follow. The horse tensed, raised its head, and then started off at a gentle canter. The horseman was Craig Wadsworth of Geneseo, New York, crack polo player and steeplechase rider. After that, the dudes and the cowboys got along fine.

San Antonians quickly got used to the sight of Colonel Roosevelt himself dashing up and down St. Mary's Street in the early morning hours, trying out the mustangs he had purchased as personal mounts. They were somewhat surprised one hot afternoon when Roosevelt halted two squadrons of dusty troopers—a considerable number of men—in front of a St. Mary's Street beer garden, turned in his saddle, and shouted, "Captains will let the men go in and drink all the beer they want, and I will pay for it!" When word got back to camp, Wood severely reprimanded his second-in-command, telling him that it was unthinkable that an officer would drink with his men. Roosevelt apologized, saying that he considered himself "the damnedest ass within ten miles of this camp."

The Rough Riders got their orders to depart for Cuba on May 24, and that night the mayor of San Antonio organized a special concert in their honor given by local musicians. The concertmaster, Carl Beck, had included in the program a number called "The Cavalry Charge," and to give it special oomph, had arranged to have a saluting cannon fired in the middle of the piece. When the gun went off someone shouted, "That's it, boys!" and hundreds of Rough Riders drew their pistols and fired into the air, and kept on firing. No one who was at that concert ever forgot it.

Texas never forgot Teddy, either. The name of Riverside Park, where the Rough Riders camped, was changed to Roosevelt Park, and a nearby street was named Roosevelt Avenue. For a while the Menger Bar was called the Roosevelt Bar. In 1902, after Roosevelt became president, a group of ranchers out in Kimble County named the town of Roosevelt after him, quite an honor for a Republican.

October 9, 2008

✦ 10 ✦

THE LIAR'S SKILL

WE ALL KNOW the type: the garrulous older gentleman who has been everywhere and done everything and is full of unwanted and usually ineffective advice. Homer pinned him down perfectly 2,700 years ago in the character of Nestor, who was fond of regaling the Greeks besieging Troy with long narratives of his own youthful successes in war and sport. Each of us knows someone like that, and we usually regard him with kindly tolerance. He is a universal.

There is a subspecies of this type, however, that may be peculiar to the American West, and that is the man whose reminiscences are so improbable as to be unbelievable, yet when challenged always has an explanation that elevates the tale to new heights of improbability. In his delightful memoir of nineteenth-century cowboy life in Montana, *We Pointed Them North*, Teddy Blue Abbott describes just such a person. He was a cowboy on a ranch where Abbott worked, an older man who had seen the elephant and heard the owl all over the West and was fond of relating his adventures to anyone who would listen. He was known as Old John. One day, according to Abbott, someone brought the mail to the main ranch house where the owner and his wife and Old John were sitting on the porch. The wife expressed delight that there were some ladies' magazines in the mail, saying that now she could see what the latest Paris fashions were.

"Paris, huh?" said Old John. "I've been to Paris."

"Oh, John, you haven't been to Paris," the owner's wife said.

"'Course I have," Old John said. "Took a beef herd there."

"How did you get them across the Atlantic Ocean?" the wife asked.

"Didn't cross no Atlantic Ocean," Old John replied. "I went around by the divide."

I once knew a man much like Old John. His name was Jack Higgins, and he was a frequent visitor to my room when I was in the hospital in Fort Worth in 1962 recovering from some broken bones. His wife was in the next room, and when he had finished his daily visit with her, he would come and see me. He was in his seventies, a tall, hawk-nosed, silver-haired countryman from Glen Rose, a little town southwest of Fort Worth. When he first dropped in he told me about his grandmother, who, although she lived in a log house with no electricity and no running water, was the wisest and kindest woman who ever lived. Her only vice was dipping snuff. Higgins was her favorite grandson.

"When Granny got old and lost her teeth," he said, "I was the only one that she would let chew the ends of the little twigs she used to dip her snuff with, get 'em rough so the snuff would stick to 'em. I've still got the last J. B. Garrett snuff can she ever dipped out of, and the last stick she used. They were in her hand when she died. I had them gold-plated and they're in my safety deposit box over at the Fort Worth National Bank."

On subsequent visits he told me about his career as a steeplejack. He was the best steeplejack that ever worked in Texas. He had painted church steeples and mounted weathervanes all the way from El Paso to Texarkana. "I can climb anything," he told me one day. "Why, when they were building that Chrysler Building in New York they couldn't find nobody to put the radio mast up. They looked all over New York and they couldn't find nobody who could do it. They called me and I went up there and had it done in a jiffy." I asked him how they happened to know about his skills way up in New York, and he said, "Why, the man that was in charge of putting that building up, Mr. Chrysler, he was from

Glen Rose. He knew me since I was a boy. My daddy used to sell him whiskey."

John Henry Faulk, Texas folklorist and storyteller, knew a man much like Jack Higgins in Austin in the 1930s. His name was Joe Whilden, and he worked for Faulk's father. Faulk loved to entertain his friends with stories about Whilden and eventually described him in an article entitled "Joe Whilden, One of the People," published by the Texas Folklore Society in 1959. Whilden was an exaggerator whose tales flew so violently in the face of fact that they were pure works of art. His specialty was the history of Austin and the surrounding area. He once told Faulk that he had known the writer O. Henry, who had left Austin in 1898 for the federal penitentiary after being convicted of bank embezzlement. "Folks are balled up on O. Henry," Whilden told Faulk. "His name wasn't O. Henry at all." Faulk, who knew that the writer's real name was William Sidney Porter, and also knew that Whilden could not read or write, was impressed. "It was Old Henry," Whilden went on. "John Old Henry. Papa hauled wood to him. He got to where he wouldn't let anybody haul his wood to him but me and he'd give me two bits extra to go get some candy. I was just a boy then."

Whilden also told Faulk that the neighborhood in south Austin called Travis Heights was the site of the last great Indian battle in America. "Yup," he said, "Stephen F. Austin led the white people, and Quanah Parker led the Indians." At this point, when recounting the story, Faulk would point out that Stephen F. Austin died in 1836 and that Quanah Parker was born about 1845. "When the battle was over and the Indians were whipped," Whilden said, "the city council of this little town here—it wasn't called Austin then, it was called Waterloo—called Stephen F. Austin in and said, 'Stephen F. Austin, we're so grateful to you for whipping the Indians that we'd like to name this town here after you.' And Stephen F. Austin said, 'No, folks, I don't want you to do that. I'd just be grateful if you'd just name that hotel over there after me.' And that's how the Stephen F. Austin Hotel got its name."

I've never been sure how much of this story is John Henry Faulk and how much is Joe Whilden, but it's hard to beat.

June 19, 2008

✣ 11 ✣

SAM BASS WAS BORN IN INDIANA

AN OLD TEXAS folksong says, *Sam met his fate at Round Rock, July the twenty-first / They filled poor Sam with rifle balls and emptied out his purse.*

This past July 21 marked the 131st anniversary of the death of the outlaw Sam Bass after being mortally wounded in a failed bank robbery in 1878 at the little town of Round Rock, just a few miles from Austin. The song about him was written a few years later, supposedly by John Denton of Gainesville. My grandmother Taylor was born in Round Rock ten months before the events it describes. Her older sister, my Aunt Carrie, who was eight at the time, always claimed that she could remember the gunfire and the men racing down the main street on horseback. Because of this, Sam Bass has always been my personal favorite Texas outlaw, and I think that the song about his career and death is one of the best of all cowboy songs.

Sam first came out to Texas, a cowboy for to be / A kinder-hearted fellow you seldom ever see.

Bass was an Indiana farm boy, but like a lot of young men at that time, he was attracted to cowboy life, and when he was seventeen he left home and headed west. He ended up in Denton, Texas, about 1872. He briefly tried cowboying and then went to work doing odd jobs for a farmer called Dad Egan, who happened to be sheriff of Denton County. Sam seemed to have a talent for friendship, but most of his friends turned out to be bad sorts.

Sam used to deal in race stock, one called the Denton mare / He ran her in scrub races, and at the county fair.

Scrub races, informal races between two horses down a quarter-mile track, were a popular form of entertainment in rural Texas. In the fall of 1874, Bass and Dad Egan's little brother Armstrong bought a fast horse named Jennie and took her on the scrub race circuit, traveling as far as San Antonio with her. Away from home she was known as "the Denton mare." She won a lot of races.

Sam left the Collins ranch in the merry month of May / With a herd of Texas cattle, the Black Hills for to see.

In San Antonio, Bass met a saloon owner, gambler, and part-time rancher named Joel Collins. They decided to buy a herd of cattle on credit and drive them to Dakota Territory. They sold them there, but instead of returning to Texas to pay off their debt, they squandered their profits in the wide-open town of Deadwood and took to robbing stagecoaches to recoup their losses. Bass later said that they were spectacularly unsuccessful, netting only a dozen peaches in one holdup.

On their way back to Texas they robbed the U. P. train / And then split up in couples and started out again.

Collins and Bass finally hit the jackpot when, with four other men, they robbed a Union Pacific train at Big Springs, Nebraska. They got $60,000 in newly-minted twenty-dollar gold pieces. They split up into pairs to elude pursuers. Collins and his partner were killed, but Bass made it back to Texas, where he hid out in the woods west of Denton and formed a new gang.

Sam's life was short in Texas, three robberies did he do / He robbed all the passenger, mail, and express cars, too.

Bass and his new gang actually held up at least two stage-coaches and four trains around Fort Worth and Dallas in the spring of 1878. There was a great public outcry. Sheriff's posses, including one led by Bass's former employer, proved ineffective, sometimes chasing each other. Governor R. B. Hubbard finally ordered the Texas Rangers to bring Sam and his boys in.

Jim had borrowed Sam's good gold and didn't want to pay / The only shot he saw was to give poor Sam away.

Major John B. Jones of the Ranger's Frontier Battalion resorted to a time-honored strategy to trap Bass. He negotiated a plea bargain with Jim Murphy, a Denton friend of Bass's who had been arrested as an accomplice in one of the train robberies and was out on bail. In spite of the song, there is no evidence that Murphy owed Bass money; he just regretted his involvement with him. Murphy agreed to join the Bass gang and report on their plans in return for the charges against him being dismissed. During the first two weeks of June 1878, while the posses were still beating the bush around Denton, Bass and his men, including Murphy, drifted south looking for a bank to rob. They finally decided on the one at Round Rock, and Murphy got a letter off to Jones alerting him.

Jones's men, assisted by some Travis and Williamson County deputy sheriffs, staked out the bank at Round Rock. According to one story, some of them hid on the second floor of the bank and bored holes in the floor so they could look down into the banking area. They never got a chance to use the peepholes. Bass and his three companions, including Murphy, made camp outside of town. On the afternoon of Friday, July 19, they rode into town, intending to case the bank and buy some tobacco and then come back and pull off the robbery on Saturday afternoon when the till would be full. Murphy lagged behind, and when the other three walked into Henry Koppel's store, a block from the bank, one of the Williamson County deputies who had been lounging in front of the store walked up behind Bass and asked him if he was carrying a pistol. Bass said yes, and shot the man. General gunfire broke out as other lawmen ran into the store, and Bass was shot through the back. He managed to mount his horse and get back to his camp, but he was captured there the next day and died the day after that—his twenty-seventh birthday.

Oh, what a scorching Jim will get when Gabriel blows his horn! / Perhaps he's gone to heaven, there's none of us can say / But if I'm right in my surmise, he's gone the other way.

Jim Murphy came to a bizarre end only two years later. He was being treated for an eye disease with a toxic eyewash that contained belladonna, some of which got into his mouth. When he swallowed a few drops of it, he died instantly.

August 27, 2009

✢ 12 ✢

MUY GRANDE RIFLES

THE OTHER DAY Glenn Moreland, Bob Miles, and I were standing in front of the Fort Davis State Bank, passing the time of day, when the subject of the Confederate cannons buried in Limpia Canyon came up. Both Miles and Moreland share my interest in the Big Bend's past, so it was a natural topic for us to be discussing. Moreland said that he and some other men were fighting a grass fire in Limpia Canyon about twenty years ago and were taking a break around the watercooler when a Mexican appeared from nowhere and asked them if they wanted to see some *muy grande rifles*—very big rifles—nearby. They told him they were too busy with the fire to go look, and he went on his way. Miles suggested that he was probably talking about the cannons that Barry Scobee had written about in his book *Old Fort Davis*. Scobee had the story from Uncle Billy Kingston, a Jeff Davis County rancher who came here in the 1880s. Kingston told Scobee that when the Sibley Brigade passed through Fort Davis in 1862 on their retreat from New Mexico to San Antonio, they were so weary and so short of draft animals that they abandoned two brass cannons, burying them about sixteen miles down Limpia Canyon from the fort. Kingston had heard the story from Adam Bradford, a cattle buyer who had accompanied the soldiers from El Paso to Fort Davis. Kingston told Scobee that he had searched for the cannons for more than forty years and never found them.

The Sibley expedition was one of the more foolhardy campaigns of the Confederacy. It was the brainchild of General Henry

Sibley, who had been an officer in the US Army in the West before the Civil War and who persuaded Jefferson Davis that a Confederate army based in Texas could capture New Mexico and use it as a springboard to conquer Colorado and California. Sibley contended that when that happened the states of Chihuahua and Sonora would leave the Mexican Republic and join the Confederacy. Davis authorized the expedition, and in November of 1861, Sibley and 3,200 men marched out of San Antonio headed for Santa Fe.

It was impossible for an army of that size to carry enough supplies to sustain it on a nine hundred-mile march, and Sibley's strategy was dependent on his army being able to buy supplies at El Paso and capture Union supplies he knew were stored at Fort Craig and Fort Union in New Mexico. None of that happened, and on top of that, Union forces destroyed what few supplies the Confederates had managed to gather when they burned the entire Confederate supply train at the Battle of Glorieta Pass in March 1862. The depleted Confederate column had no choice but to give up the whole enterprise and straggle home on starvation rations.

The artillery that they had taken with them, augmented by a Union battery that they had captured along the way, proved to be a burden on the march home and some of it was abandoned. Its disposition became the subject of a web of folklore that is still thriving in the Southwest, as my conversation in front of the Fort Davis State Bank proves. Sibley buffs have engaged in the sport of cannon-counting for the past fifty years, and there are stories about buried cannons all the way from Albuquerque to San Antonio. The problem is that while there is a newspaper account that describes the remnants of the army arriving in San Antonio with six cannons, no one can agree on exactly how many they started out from Santa Fe with. It is a matter of record that they buried eight in the middle of the night on the plaza in Albuquerque and that in 1889, Trevanion Teel, Sibley's chief of artillery, supervised their exhumation. Six of the cannons ended up in museums in Colorado and New Mexico; it is not clear what happened to the other two. One of them may have become the famous McGinty cannon, which was used in the 1890s by an El Paso men's club to announce its revels and which was borrowed by sympathizers of Francisco Madero to play a minor role in the Mexican Revolution. That cannon now reposes at Eastwood High School in El Paso — maybe. There are those who say that the real McGinty cannon was given to a World War II scrap drive, and others who say it was not one of the Sibley cannons to start with.

There have been persistent rumors of a Sibley cannon buried near Socorro, New Mexico. These seem to have their origin in an entry of the journal of A. B. Peticolas, one of Sibley's men who on April 19, 1862, after describing a march down a long canyon, mentions "the point where we left the canion [sic]." From my reading of the journal, it is pretty clear to me that Peticolas was no champion speller and was referring to leaving the canyon and not the cannon. But in the 1950s, some ranch hands moving cattle in the area found a cannon half-buried in an arroyo. They brought it into Socorro, and it was displayed in a local historian's front yard until the late 1970s, when it disappeared. It turned out to have been stolen from the yard by an Albuquerque man who used it to make a mold from which he cast several reproduction cannons. He salted those around the base of Ladron Peak and then charged Civil War buffs hefty sums to lead them to the fake cannon. The man eventually went to prison and the original cannon was returned to its owner, but there seems to be no hard evidence that it was one of Sibley's.

I once saw a genuine Sibley expedition relic. When I lived in Round Top, I knew an old bachelor farmer named Leslie Kneip, and I was visiting with him on his front porch one day when he said he wanted to show me something. He brought out a mess of oily rags and unwrapped a Model 1851 Colt Navy revolver, which he said his grandfather had carried to New Mexico and back during the Civil War. While I was admiring it he added, "My grandfather wasn't sure these revolvers would work, so he took this along, too." He pulled from the rags a huge old German flintlock pistol that must have been a hundred years old in 1861. It wasn't a cannon, but it was nearly as big as one, and almost as heavy. And definitely genuine.

June 18, 2009

✥ 13 ✥

THE TEXAS SIGNERS

I CANNOT LET the month of March go by without mentioning the fifty-nine men who came together in a drafty, unfinished building at Washington-on-the-Brazos 173 years ago this month to declare Texas an independent republic. In the seventeen days that they met together there, they also wrote a constitution for the new republic, organized an ad interim government, and appointed one of their number, Sam Houston, as commander-in-chief of the new republic's pitiful little army. They convened on March 1, 1836, and adjourned early on the morning of March 17, panicked by reports of Santa Anna's approaching army.

It is interesting to compare the fifty-nine men who signed the Texas Declaration of Independence with the fifty-six who signed a similar document at Philadelphia sixty years earlier on July 4, 1776. The Philadelphia signers were members of a Continental Congress that had convened a year earlier, and they were the leading men of Great Britain's North American colonies: lawyers, bankers, merchants, and planters, all substantial citizens. Many of their names have reverberated down through American history because of their subsequent deeds—John Adams, Thomas Jefferson, John Hancock, Richard Henry Lee, Benjamin Rush. The men who met at Washington-on-the-Brazos in 1836 had been elected from their various districts the month before. Most of them were relative newcomers to Texas and, after coming together to create a new nation, few of them played leading roles in its history. The majority of them went back home and picked up their plows and settled into roles as local patriarchs. Sam Houston, Samuel Maverick, and Jose Antonio Navarro carved out places for themselves in the history textbooks, but most of the others had to be satisfied with having a county somewhere in West Texas or a public school in their hometown named for them. Who has ever heard of Thomas J. Gazley, Benjamin Goodrich, or John Byrom?

The delegates to the 1775 Continental Congress were cultured, educated men from cities on the Eastern Seaboard. The men who attended the convention of 1836 were representative of the frontier Texas environment from which they came; in other words, they were a pretty rough bunch. Robert Potter, a delegate from Nacogdoches, had served prison time in North Carolina for castrating two men that he suspected of dallying with his wife (this form of punishment became known in Texas as "potterizing") and had been expelled from the North Carolina legislature for cheating at cards. Potter later served as Secretary of the Navy of the Republic of Texas on the strength of having been a midshipman in the US Navy when he was fifteen. He eventually met his end at the hands of a mob that surrounded his home on Caddo Lake during the Regulator-Moderator feud in 1842.

Some of the delegates were literally transients. Jesse Badgett came from Arkansas to Texas in the fall of 1835 to join the revolutionary army and enlisted in Travis's command at the Alamo. On February 1, 1836, his fellow soldiers elected him to the convention along with Samuel Maverick. A month later he signed the Declaration of Independence and then went back to Arkansas, leaving others to deal with the consequences of his act. He was interviewed by a Little Rock newspaper on April 12, 1836, giving an account of the fall of the Alamo, and then disappeared from history.

There was one exception to these frontiersmen. Lorenzo de Zavala, the delegate from Harrisburg, was a Mexican aristocrat, born into a landowning family in Yucatán. He was a man of the world who had served as a delegate to both the Spanish Parliament and the Mexican Congress and had been Secretary of the Treasury of the Republic of Mexico and the Mexican Minister to France.

He was fluent in Spanish, English, and French, and he impressed everyone at the convention with his knowledge, his bearing, and his easy manners. His fellow delegates elected him ad interim vice president of the Republic, and he would undoubtedly have gone on to a distinguished career in Texas had he not caught pneumonia crossing Buffalo Bayou in an open boat and died in November 1836.

My favorite delegate is Collin McKinney of Pecan Point in North Texas, a through-and-through frontiersman who at the age of seventy rode horseback through freezing rain for a week to reach Washington-on-the-Brazos. McKinney was born in New Jersey in 1766, a subject of King George III. As a child he had moved with his family to Virginia, and then on west to Kentucky, and then to Arkansas. In the early 1830s, he brought his wife and his half a dozen children, and their children, to Texas and settled just south of the Red River, in an area that was claimed by both Arkansas and Mexico. After signing the declaration, he served in the first three congresses of the republic, riding horseback from the Red River to the various capitals once a year. He became a vehement opponent of Sam Houston, whom he regarded as entirely too well-disposed toward the Cherokees and whose flamboyant personal characteristics he could not abide.

Some time in the 1840s, McKinney and his children founded the community of Mantua in what is now Collin County, and my great-grandfather Taylor's parents joined them there. One of my grandfather's sisters married a grandson of Collin McKinney, bringing into the Taylor family circle a somewhat alarming woman known as Aunt Molly McKinney, who I think must have been one of Collin McKinney's daughters-in-law. When my grandmother Taylor was selling china at Stripling's Department Store in Fort Worth in the 1920s, she dreaded Aunt Molly's occasional shopping trips to town because she knew two things about her: Aunt Molly dipped snuff, and while she would not dip it in the store, she always had a tell-tale dribble of brown liquid on the side of her chin, and she kept her money secured in the top of her stocking. When it came time to pay her shopping bill, she would prop her foot on a chair, hike up her skirt, and remove a roll of bills from her garter. She was a nineteenth-century country woman, and was as out of place in a sophisticated Fort Worth department store as Lorenzo de Zavala had been at Washington-on-the-Brazos.

March 19, 2009

✣ 14 ✣

THE VILLAIN OF SAN JACINTO

THIS SATURDAY will be the 171st anniversary of the Battle of San Jacinto, the eighteen-minute fight that gained Texas her independence from Mexico. That battle created Texas's most enduring hero, Sam Houston, a larger-than-life figure whose larger-than-life statue (it is sixty-seven feet high) towers over Interstate 45 at Huntsville. But what about the man who lost the battle, Antonio Lopez de Santa Anna, who was as remarkable in his own way as Houston? He is the villain of Texas history, responsible for the Alamo and the Goliad massacre, and there are no statues to him anywhere. His name continues to fascinate, and stories about him have resonated down through time.

One of the remarkable things about Santa Anna was his resilience, and another was his duplicity. He served as president of Mexico eleven times at four different periods. He was first elected in 1833 as a liberal, pledged to support a federal constitution modeled on that of the United States. As soon as he took office he announced that he had decided that he was a conservative and scrapped that constitution, an action that helped cause the Texas Revolution. He was president again from 1841 to 1844, when he was overthrown and sent into exile in Cuba. During the Mexican War, he promised agents of President Polk that if the US government would get him back into the presidency, he would arrange a peace treaty favorable to the US. Instead, he led an army against Zachary Taylor's troops and was soundly defeated, resulting in his second exile, this time to Jamaica. He came back again in 1853 and stayed in office just long enough to bankrupt Mexico and declare himself president for life with the title of "Serene

Highness"; in 1855 he went into permanent exile and lived most of the rest of his life in Cuba, Colombia, and New York. He was allowed to return to Mexico in 1874 and died two years later, penniless and blind.

Santa Anna may have died in obscurity, but stories about him continued to circulate down through the twentieth century. When I lived in Round Top, over in Fayette County, I heard a good deal about his vest. It seems that one of his captors after the Battle of San Jacinto was a Round Top boy, Joel Robison. Robison and some other men found Santa Anna wandering on the prairie after the battle, dressed as a civilian. Robison, not knowing who he was, took him up behind him on his horse and brought him into the Texan camp. Before he was recognized and hustled off to Houston's tent, Santa Anna gave Robison his vest, a gray cloth vest with brass buttons. For the next seventy years, every young man in Round Top who got married wore that vest at his wedding. It disappeared, or perhaps disintegrated, about 1910.

Then there is the matter of Santa Anna's artificial leg. The dictator's right leg was amputated below the knee in 1838, after it was shattered by a French cannonball during the bombardment of Veracruz. He had two cork legs made by a North American cabinetmaker, Charles Bartlett. They were quite handsome, equipped with ball bearing joints and terminating in leather ankle boots. When soldiers from the Fourth Illinois Volunteer Regiment captured Santa Anna's coach at the Mexican War Battle of Cerro Gordo in 1847, they found his uneaten roasted chicken dinner, a chest containing $20,000, and his spare cork leg. There is a fanciful contemporary lithograph of the scene, showing one of the soldiers waving the leg at the retreating Santa Anna as Zachary Taylor and his troops charge by in the foreground. The soldiers, who were from Pekin, Illinois, ate the chicken dinner and turned the money chest over to the paymaster, but they kept the cork leg and eventually took it back to Pekin, where First Sergeant Sam Rhodes displayed it in his home. He and his fellow veterans Abraham

Waldron and John Gill traveled around the Illinois countryside with it, exhibiting it in saloons and charging patrons a dime to handle it. It eventually found its way to the Illinois State Capitol Building, where it was on public display for nearly a century, and now it can be seen at the Illinois State Military Museum at Camp Lincoln in Springfield.

Most historians agree that Santa Anna was born in Veracruz in 1794, but there is a Kentucky folktale that holds that he was actually born in Kentucky, the illegitimate son of Nathan Saunders of Frankfort and an Indian woman. When he was a young man, his father secured a West Point appointment for him, but he ran afoul of the regulations and disappeared, never to be heard of again. After the Battle of San Jacinto, when Santa Anna was being escorted to Washington to see Andrew Jackson, his party stopped at a Frankfort tavern for the night. Word got out that Santa Anna was in town and a mob of angry Kentuckians assembled in the street, intent on lynching him. When the mob's leaders got into the tavern, however, they recognized Santa Anna as their childhood playmate and kinsman. He explained to them that when he left West Point he had gone to Mexico, learned Spanish, changed his name, and risen in the Mexican Army to his present position. They agreed to spare his life and to keep his secret in order to protect their state's honor, and the mob dispersed. The writer Irwin S. Cobb, who was related to the Saunders family, tells this story in his 1941 autobiography, *Exit Laughing*, adding that his grandfather Saunders was convinced that there was no truth in it. So am I.

There may be something, however, in another Santa Anna story. According to this one, when the general was in exile in New York in the late 1860s he got involved in a scheme to import *chicle* from Mexico and use it to manufacture a substitute for the rubber that was used on buggy tires. He was working with an inventor, Thomas Adams, who was unable to turn the *chicle* into a rubber substitute, but noticed that Santa Anna enjoyed chewing on a little ball of it. Adams experimented further with the *chicle* and eventually developed something he called Chiclets. He opened the world's first chewing gum factory and the rest is history. If Santa Anna was responsible for chewing gum, he was a very great villain indeed.

April 19, 2007

✤ 15 ✤

FERDINAND LINDHEIMER,
FRONTIER JOURNALIST

EARLY IN DECEMBER, I found myself in New Braunfels, Texas, for the first time in about thirty years. The last time I was there, New Braunfels was a quiet little town where you could still hear people speaking German on Seguin Street on a Saturday morning. Now it has a population of over fifty thousand and is a suburb of San Antonio. One thing that has not changed, however, is the Naeglin Bakery, which has been in business at 129 Seguin since 1870 and has the largest stock of irresistible pastries in Texas. I stopped in there for coffee and a mid-morning snack, which I will not describe except to say that it was made out of eggs, flour, and sugar, and I ate only half of it. While I was sitting on the bakery's patio enjoying my forbidden fruit, I became aware that a steady stream of small children was coming out of the bakery's back door, each clutching a sugar-covered pastry in a paper napkin. I asked one young fellow who appeared to be about eight why he and his friends were not in school and he replied, his eyes shining, "We're on a field trip." Only in New Braunfels, I thought, would a school make a field trip to a bakery.

Across the alley from the patio was a two-story brick building whose side was covered with a mural paying tribute to one of New Braunfels's most distinguished citizens, Ferdinand Jacob Lindheimer, botanist and editor of the *Neu-Braunfelser Zeitung*. New Braunfels was founded in 1845 by a minor German prince called Carl of Solms-Braunfels, who was the commissioner-general of a company established to bring German immigrants to Texas; for many years the first language of most of the town's residents was

German. When Lindheimer started the *Zeitung* in 1852, it was a bilingual newspaper. The German section was finally dropped in 1957, which says something about the durability of the German language in Texas.

Whoever painted the mural depicted Lindheimer as a kindly, white-bearded, twinkly-eyed old gentleman standing beside a printing press, a sort of Santa Claus in a leather apron. The image made me think that the artist probably did not know much about Lindheimer, who was one of those remarkable Germans who came to Texas in the mid-nineteenth century and made places like New Braunfels and Fredericksburg islands of European culture on the Texas frontier. Frederick Law Olmsted, a New York journalist who visited Texas about the time that Lindheimer founded the *Zeitung*, reported spending the night near New Braunfels with a German settler whose bookcase was half full of sweet potatoes and half full of volumes of Cicero, and I have always thought that was the perfect metaphor for the Texas German settlements. Lindheimer, who was born into a middle-class family in Frankfurt am Main in 1801, received a classical education at three German universities and taught at the Bunsen Institute in Frankfort before coming to the United States in 1834.

Lindheimer left Germany because the Bunsen Institute, which was a preparatory school for boys established by Georg Bunsen, was a hotbed of revolutionaries determined to overthrow the reactionary monarchs who ruled the various German states and establish a unified, democratic Germany. The school was actually a kind of commune. Students and teachers wore long hair and beards, dressed alike in loose-fitting clothes derived from peasant costumes, and addressed each other with the informal "*du.*" In 1833 Bunsen and his teachers and students participated in an armed riot in Frankfurt in which seven faculty members were arrested for sedition. Lindheimer always claimed that he did not take part in the riot, but the experience marked him for life. He broke all ties with his family, slipped away from Frankfurt, and turned up, along with some of his former Bunsen colleagues, in a German utopian settlement in Bellville, Illinois. For the rest of his life, he inveighed against compromise and submission to authority.

Lindheimer first came to Texas in 1836 to fight in the Texas Revolution. He later said that he came because of his hatred of political oppression in general and Antonio Lopez de Santa Anna in particular (he had lived in Santa Anna's Mexico for a year and a half before coming to Texas). Lindheimer's company was stationed on Galveston Island, and although they hastened to join Houston's army at San Jacinto, they missed the battle by one day.

Lindheimer had been a botanist since his university days, and after his discharge from the army, he stayed in Texas to collect botanical specimens, which he sent to Georg Engelmann in St. Louis. Engelmann arranged for him to receive a salary for his work, and for the next few years he traveled around Texas in a two-wheeled cart loaded down with pressing paper, preparing specimens and sending them to Engelmann's herbarium in St. Louis. The Missouri Botanical Garden still has these specimens, labeled in Lindheimer's precise handwriting.

When Prince Solms-Braunfels came to Texas, Lindheimer signed up as a guide for his colonists, which is how he came to settle in New Braunfels in 1848. The newspaper he published there must be unique among Texas newspapers because Lindheimer viewed his task as editor as being not only to inform but to instruct his readers. He wrote long articles replete with classical references; in one of them he compared the Comanches' raids of local ranches to Odysseus's and Diomedes's theft of the horses of King Rhesus and Hercules's robbery of the children of Geyron. One of his favorite themes was the conflict between religion and science, a conflict in which he was firmly on the side of science. He compared scientists to Spartan soldiers in battle, "singing the battle-song of Tyrtaeus, 'Beautiful it is to die in battle, fighting in the front rank.'" Everyone who knew him and wrote about him commented on his implacable hostility toward organized religion. In his editorials, he referred to the clergy as "spiritual robbers," "salary-priests," and "Levites." The epithets sound much nastier in German.

Lindheimer died in 1879, but he left Texans a lasting legacy, one that is appropriate to his combative personality. He gave his name to the Texas prickly pear, *Opuntia lindheimeri*.

January 24, 2008

❖ 16 ❖

REAL COWBOYS DON'T HAVE
TIME TO SING

I EXPERIENCED my first great disappointment in life at the age of seven, when I went from Washington, DC, to spend the summer at my great-uncles' ranch in Texas and discovered that none of the cowboys there could sing. I had learned all about cowboys by watching the Saturday afternoon movies at the Shirlington Theatre, and I knew that a guitar was as indispensable to their work as a pistol, a rope, and a horse. But neither of my great-uncles nor any of the men who worked for them could sing, and there was not a guitar in sight. They could ride and rope and Uncle Sid even kept a pistol in the glove compartment of his pickup, but without guitars how could they be real cowboys?

I was a victim of the singing cowboy myth, a joint creation of Hollywood and a folklorist named John A. Lomax. Now let me say right up front that I am sure that some nineteenth-century working cowboys were musical. In fact, another one of my great-uncles, Gus Staples, is mentioned in J. Marvin Hunter's book, *The Trail Drivers of Texas*, as being a popular man on trail drives because he could play the fiddle. Some cowboys undoubtedly sang to themselves on night guard, probably humming familiar hymns or wordless tunes that sounded something like Eddie Arnold's "Cattle Call." I will even concede that there are some genuine cowboy ballads from the nineteenth century, such as "The Old Chisholm Trail," about which J. Frank Dobie said that there was a verse for every mile of the trail and that "most of them were unmailable." The recorded versions have been considerably cleaned up.

I will submit that most popular cowboy songs did not begin life on the trail, but were commercial productions that were first popularized by radio singers and then found their way into the movies. Fort Davis rancher John G. Prude's favorite, the rollicking song about a disastrous bronco ride called "The Strawberry Roan," is a good example. The words were written by cowboy poet and rodeo promoter Curley Fletcher and were first published as a poem in the Globe, Arizona, *Arizona Record* in 1915. No one knows who set them to music, but the song became the theme song of Romaine Lowdermilk and the Arizona Ramblers, who performed in the nightclub at the Arizona Biltmore in Phoenix and over Phoenix radio station KTAR in the 1930s. In 1933, Ken Maynard sang it in a film called *The Strawberry Roan*, and from there it passed into popular culture. By the late 1930s it was being collected as a folk song.

It was the folklorist John A. Lomax who gave the singing cowboy his start. Lomax, who grew up on a ranch in Bosque County, became interested in collecting cowboy songs when he was teaching at Texas A&M in the early 1900s. Inspired by ballad collectors who took wax-cylinder recording machines into the Appalachians to track down old English ballads, he hauled a similar machine to cattlemen's conventions and asked the older attendees to sing into it for him. He also sent a form letter to every newspaper editor in the West, asking for examples of "ballads of the cattle trade." Only fifty-four of the hundreds of song recordings that he made have survived, and, of those, only a few are songs about cowboy life—most of them are popular songs of the 1880s and '90s—but the responses of the newspaper editors are all in the John A. Lomax papers at the University of Texas at Austin. They consist largely of poems written for newspaper publication, many of them clipped directly from the newspaper. In 1910, Lomax published *Cowboy Songs*, a book containing 112 song texts but only fourteen tunes. In the introduction he claimed that the songs in the book were made up on the trail, with all of the cowboys in a camp contributing verses. Perhaps he thought they were.

Cowboy singers came into their own when radio became a popular entertainment medium in the 1920s. It was a poor station, no matter how far east it might be, that could not boast a Lonesome Cowboy or a Sagebrush Sam, and these performers turned to Lomax's book for their material. Sometimes they composed their own tunes; sometimes they used tunes to which professional composers had set Lomax's words, such as the English composer Liza Lehmann's tunes for "The Night-Herding Song" and "The Skew-Ball Black." What is certain is that they did not sing the few genuine cowboy songs that had been sent to Lomax (but not published by him) because the words would have scorched the air waves. Radio singers increased their popularity by making records, and again they turned to Lomax. When Carl T. Sprague, the Texas A&M track coach who is regarded as the first cowboy recording star, made his first record for Victor in 1925, he chose D. J. O'Malley's poem "When the Work's All Done This Fall," right out of Lomax.

The first cowboy movie stars were silent because the first movies were silent. They tended to be athletic cowboys in the tradition of Buffalo Bill's Wild West and the hundreds of other wild west shows that imitated it, men like Tom Mix and Bronco Billy Anderson, whose fancy riding, roping, and shooting tricks made an easy transition from the circus arena to film. But in 1927 movies began to talk, and the singing cowboy stepped out from behind the radio mike and onto the sound stage. The two most famous, of course, were Gene Autry, Oklahoma's Singing Cowboy from radio station KVOO in Tulsa, and Roy Rogers (born Leonard Slye), from the Sons of the Pioneers on station KFWB in Los Angeles. There were others, and their repertoire began to include compositions by the Tin Pan Alley stars like Cole Porter ("Don't Fence Me In"), Johnny Mercer ("I'm an Old Cowhand from the Rio Grande"), and Frank Loesser ("I've Got Spurs that Jingle Jangle Jingle"). We are a long ways from the cow camp, folks.

All of this is by way of an explanation as to why my great-uncles and the men who worked for them did not play guitars and sing cowboy songs—they were too busy trying to run a ranch.

August 27, 2008

✥ 17 ✥

ROY W. ALDRICH,
THE ERUDITE RANGER

NOT LONG AGO I was prowling around the shelves of the Wildenthal Library at Sul Ross State University, which I often do when I have gone over there to look something up and have some spare time on my hands, and I stumbled on a whole clutch of English fox-hunting memoirs, books with titles like *Trencher and Kennel: Some Famous Yorkshire Packs*, published in London in 1927, and *The Eighth Duke of Badminton and the Badminton Hunt*, London, 1901. These seemed to me to be odd volumes to encounter in the library of a West Texas cow college until I remembered Texas Ranger Captain Roy W. Aldrich, whose library and papers were acquired by Sul Ross in 1958. Then it all made sense.

Roy Aldrich was undoubtedly the most literate Texas Ranger in the history of the Ranger force, and surely one of the most intellectually curious. By the time of his death in 1955, he had assembled a library of ten thousand volumes, which took up the entire second floor of his large Austin home. The first floor was stuffed with collections of Indian pottery, arrowheads and stone artifacts, horns, spurs, firearms, and other Western memorabilia. The twenty-acre grounds of that home, which was out east of town on Manor Road, included several gardens of native plants and a private zoo. Aldrich was an omnivorous reader who spent most of his salary on books, as the receipts in his papers show. The largest part of his library consisted of volumes on Texas and the Southwest, but he also formed respectable collections on ornithology, natural history, hunting and outdoor life (thus the English fox-hunting memoirs), and travel. He also collected erotica, racy little volumes with titles like *Spanked Ladies.*

Aldrich's life was as varied and colorful as his library. He was born in 1869 in Illinois and grew up in Golden City, Missouri, where his father owned a bank. He never went to school, but was educated at home by his mother, who had been a teacher. At seventeen he left home and went to Idaho, where he worked as a lumberjack and steamboat hand. In the 1890s, Aldrich spent some time as a horse trader and deputy sheriff in Oklahoma Territory, as the owner of a coffee plantation in Mexico, and as a stagecoach driver in Arizona Territory. During the Spanish-American War, he served with a Missouri volunteer regiment in the Philippines, and when that war was over, he took a load of horses to South Africa for the British Army's use during the Boer War. He came to Texas in 1907 and went into the real estate business, first in Corpus Christi and then in San Antonio. But when the border troubles broke out in 1915, he couldn't stay away from the action, and at the age of forty-five, he joined the Texas Rangers as a private in Company A, stationed in Rio Grande City. His talents were quickly recognized, and by 1919 he had been promoted to captain and appointed Quartermaster and Paymaster of the Rangers, a position he held for twenty-eight years until his retirement in 1947.

Aldrich first came to the Big Bend on Ranger business in 1920 and returned many times over the years, sometimes on official business and sometimes to collect plants and natural history specimens. He made many friends here, including Sul Ross President Horace Morelock. In 1940, Morelock started trolling for Aldrich's library and collections, hoping to bring them to Sul Ross. He wrote Aldrich a letter describing the new museum building on the campus, saying that it was "fireproof and had steel doors, every one of which is kept locked." He pointed out that ex-Rangers James B. Gillett and Everett Townsend had recently donated their collections to the museum, adding that "we are specializing in this type of material." When Aldrich failed to take the bait, Morelock got Harry Anthony DeYoung, who ran the Sul Ross summer art program, to paint Aldrich's portrait on horseback to hang in the museum. He persuaded a graduate student to write Aldrich's biography for her master's thesis. Aldrich donated several items to the museum, and told Morelock several times that he wanted his library to eventually go to the college, but he could not bear to part with his books during his lifetime. He died in 1955 and left his entire estate, including his library, to his housekeeper, a Mrs. R. M. Riley of Austin.

Sul Ross's friends immediately mobilized to bring Aldrich's library to Alpine. Dudley Dobie, a San Marcos bookseller and a longtime friend of Aldrich, offered to inventory and appraise the books. Mrs. Riley agreed to sell them for their $50,000 appraised value. Hallie Stillwell and Virginia Madison set out in a Sul Ross station wagon to raise the money. It was in the middle of a drought and no one in West Texas had any spare cash. In a letter to the Alpine *Avalanche*, Stillwell told how they drove all over West Texas and came back to Alpine two days before the deadline with pledges for $47,000. That night, she and Madison ran into Alpine rancher H. L. Kokernot, Jr. at the American Legion Hall and told him their story. He reached into his pocket, pulled out his checkbook, and wrote them a check for $3,000. Because of his impulsive generosity, the collection was in the bag.

Today, Aldrich's books form the core of the Texas and Southwestern Collection of the Wildenthal Library. Dudley Dobie reportedly culled out the erotica before the collection arrived on the campus, but one volume slipped through, a little book entitled A *Chimpanzee and Two Girls*, published by the French Arts Press in 1933. You have to ask at the desk of the Archives of the Big Bend to see it. Captain Roy Aldrich was indeed a man of spacious tastes.

March 15, 2007

✣ 18 ✣

WIGFALL VAN SICKLE,
THE SAGE OF ALPINE

JUDGE WIGFALL VAN SICKLE of
Alpine was not only a distin-
guished jurist with a preposterous name, he was an accomplished
raconteur and is responsible for many of the Big Bend's best-
known tales.

For example, the story about the steer branded "murder,"
which found its way into half a dozen books including J. Frank
Dobie's *Longhorns*, seems to have started with Judge Van Sickle.
According to Barry Scobee's pamphlet, *The Steer Branded Murder*,
Van Sickle first published the story in the *Galveston News* about
1896. In order to give the tale a ring of veracity, Van Sickle
claimed that he had encountered the animal one night on the
prairie while traveling between Alpine and Fort Stockton, roped
him and tried to brand him, and then discovered the letters M-U-
R-D-E-R branded on his side.

Wigfall Van Sickle was born in Henderson, Texas, in 1863 and
was named after Louis T. Wigfall, a fire-eating secessionist who
was a Confederate senator from Texas. Van Sickle came to Alpine
in 1885 as a schoolteacher, read law, was admitted to the bar, and
in 1888 at the age of twenty-five, was elected county judge of
newly-organized Brewster County. Hallie Stillwell, in her memoir,
I'll Gather My Geese, says that her husband Roy told her that Van
Sickle was responsible for getting the state legislature to abolish
Foley and Buchel counties in 1897, thus depriving Marathon of
the opportunity to become a county seat. If this is true, he left no
paper trail. However, he was elected to the legislature in 1900 and
served two terms.

After that he settled down in Alpine and became the Big Bend's best-known lawyer. He mastered the peculiar and occasionally irregular land surveys of the Big Bend and specialized in land law. He got his feet wet in these matters by losing a civil suit involving a renumbered section of land to Howard E. Perry, owner of the Chisos Mining Company at Terlingua. Perry was so impressed by Van Sickle's abilities that he subsequently retained him as the mining company's attorney and his own personal advisor. Van Sickle once described the outcome of the case in a letter: "Seeing the intrepid quality of the owner of the mine and finding out that he would rather have a fight than a frolic the writer went to his side of the fence where he has been stationed on the watch tower as trumpeter of the territory." Van Sickle also became the trumpeter for the Southern Pacific and the Galveston, Harrisburg & San Antonio railroads, looking after their extensive landholdings in the Big Bend.

He also practiced criminal law and became famous for his ability to sway juries no matter how damning the facts in the case appeared. In 1912, he defended rancher Jim Gillespie who, after several months of making threats against a neighboring rancher, walked into the Alpine post office one morning and shot him six times in front of a crowd of witnesses. Van Sickle obtained three hung juries for Gillespie in three separate trials. A fourth trial was pending when Gillespie was killed by an irate husband in New Mexico.

Sometime in the 1930s, a student of Clifford Casey's at Sul Ross State University made a record of Van Sickle's argument to a jury in a goat-rustling case. The document is now in the Archives of the Big Bend and it is a fine example of Van Sickle's jury technique. The defendant was a desperately poor man with eleven children, living in a three-room house in the Chisos Mountains, who was charged with butchering a wealthy neighbor's goat. Van Sickle first determined that the jury included both a Confederate veteran and a veteran of World War I who had served in France.

In cross-examining the owner of the butchered goat, he elicited the facts that the man had been born in Germany and that he owned thousands of goats. In his summation to the jury, he began by stating that he realized his client was probably going to prison for trying to feed his starving family. Then he launched into a speech that included references to Robert E. Lee's army living on nothing but parched corn during the winter of 1864 and the German shelling of civilians in Paris in World War I. According to the student, Van Sickle's client was "a hard-bitten man who had never shed a tear in his life," but at a prearranged signal, as Van Sickle described the dismal fate of the eleven children if their father went to prison, the defendant pulled out a handkerchief which Van Sickle had filled with chopped onions and burst into tears. The jury acquitted him.

One of Van Sickle's courtroom arguments became a footnote in American literary history. In 1933, the Chicago author Nelson Algren, still an unknown, was riding freight trains through the Southwest, gathering material for a novel about hobos. He stopped off in Alpine, and when he decided to move on, he took a typewriter from a Sul Ross State University office with him. He was arrested and charged with theft of state property. When his case came to trial, Wigfall Van Sickle was appointed to defend him. It appeared to be an open-and-shut case, since Algren had signed a confession, but Van Sickle did his best. He entered a plea of not guilty and proceeded to argue that it was a principle of English common law that a mechanic was entitled to the tools of his trade, and since Algren was a writer without a typewriter, he was entitled to one, so taking it was not really theft. The jury found Algren guilty but recommended leniency, and the judge gave him a probated sentence and ordered him to leave Texas within twenty-four hours. It is a shame that Van Sickle did not live to see Algren win the 1950 National Book Award for *The Man With the Golden Arm*.

June 21, 2007

✥ 19 ✥

THE MEXICAN REVOLUTION
IN TEXAS

EVERYONE IN TEXAS knows stories about the way that the Mexican Revolution of 1910-1930 spilled over the border. These stories are usually about raids across the river that resulted in bloodshed on this side, such as the Glenn Springs raid in 1916 and the Brite Ranch raid in 1917. My own mother lived in Kingsville as a girl and vividly remembered her terror when news came one Sunday morning in 1915 that Aniceto Pizaña and his men had derailed the train between Kingsville and Brownsville and murdered the engineer. The engineer's daughter was her best friend.

What does not find its way into the stories is that the violence flowed both ways across the permeable border. There was the Great Marfa Payroll Robbery, for instance. In July 1919, Captain Palma, a Mexican Army paymaster, got off the train at Marfa with a briefcase containing $22,600, the payroll for the Mexican Army garrison at Ojinaga. Because of the difficulty of reaching Ojinaga from Ciudad Juarez, Palma and his escort of four soldiers had crossed the border and taken the train east from El Paso. At Marfa they arranged for a local man, Andy Barker, to drive them to Presidio, where they intended to cross the border again, pay off the garrison, and return to El Paso. They started off from Marfa after dark, but about two miles south of town, they found the road blocked by a Ford automobile parked across it. Several men with guns jumped out of it, grabbed the briefcase from Captain Palma, got back in their car and took off into the darkness. Because of its international implications, the FBI investigated the case, as did the

Texas Rangers. Both agencies gave the district attorney's office a list of suspects, which included Andy Barker and the sheriff's brother. After a brief period of indirection during which the sheriff tried to throw suspicion on a group of soldiers at Camp Marfa, the district attorney tried to bring indictments against the men on the list, but the grand jury refused to indict some of Marfa's best-known citizens, and the robbery is officially still unsolved.

Then there was the killing of General Pascual Orozco on the Love Ranch in Hudspeth County. Orozco was one of the original leaders of the 1910 revolution against Porfirio Díaz, but after Díaz's fall, Orozco parted ways with his fellow revolutionaries and threw his support behind Victoriano Huerta, a former general in Díaz's army who became president in a counter-revolutionary coup in 1913. Huerta was soon overthrown in turn and went into exile, but he tried to make a comeback. Orozco traveled around the United States buying guns for him and enlisted the support of many conservative Texas businessmen and ranchers. In June 1915, both Orozco and Huerta were arrested by federal officers at Newman, New Mexico, taken to El Paso, and charged with violating the Neutrality Act. They made bond, and the mayor of El Paso offered to defend them in court, but a few days later, Orozco jumped bail and disappeared into the Big Bend. A few weeks later, he and three companions, all armed, rode up to the isolated Dick Love ranch house south of Sierra Blanca and asked the cook there to fix them breakfast. While they were eating it, they saw a car coming up the road toward the house and, spooked, jumped on their horses and headed for the Eagle Mountains. The car contained Love and some of his cowboys, come to start the fall roundup. When the cook told Love that there were four strange armed Mexicans on the place, Love jumped to the conclusion that they were bandits and called the sheriff at Sierra Blanca to get a posse together. The posse tracked Orozco and his men through the Eagle Mountains for two days, finally pinned them down in a canyon, and killed all four of them. It was only when they found a watch with the initials "P. O." on one of the dead men that they realized whom they had killed.

The fluid nature of the border in those years is nowhere better illustrated than by the words used by Sheriff Amador Sanchez of Laredo in applying for a presidential pardon after he was convicted of smuggling guns across the river to assist General Bernardo Reyes in 1911. In a tone of outrage he wrote to President Taft that "This custom of purchasing arms, horses, and munitions of war along the Rio Grande for revolutionaries in Mexico has prevailed ever since I was a boy, and no one has ever been prosecuted for it until now." Crossing the border for illegal purposes is nothing new in Texas. In fact, you might almost say it is a tradition.

October 20, 2005

✥ 20 ✥

HOW LEIGHTON KNIPE LEFT HIS
MARK ON MARFA

VISITORS TO MARFA this past
year (and there have been a
lot of them) always comment on the four particularly handsome
buildings along the west side of Highland Avenue: the First
Christian Church, the Paisano Hotel, the Brite Building, and the
Marfa National Bank. The Paisano was designed by the well-
known El Paso firm of Trost & Trost, but the other three buildings
are the work of a much more obscure architect, Leighton Green
Knipe. They are built in a style that is a combination of Spanish-
Pueblo Revival and art deco, and they are very fine buildings
indeed.

Knipe came to the Big Bend in the mid-1920s and worked in
Marfa under the patronage of rancher Lucas Brite for fifteen years,
but he has proved to be an elusive fellow to learn anything about.
Lee Bennett remembers him as a diminutive man with a little
goatee who lived by himself in an apartment that he rented from
her mother, and Jane Brite White recalls that he smoked little
Between the Acts cigars, that she and her sister called him Uncle
Billy, and that he had a scientific bent and helped her grandfather
drill some oil wells on the Brite Ranch that turned out to be dry
holes, but beyond that he did not make much impression on
Marfa's collective memory. Both Bennett and White have small
pewter statues that he made of them when they were little girls.
Knipe died in Marfa in 1941, and his body was shipped to
California for burial.

The odd thing is that when I started looking into his career, I
discovered that he is something of a cult figure to architectural

enthusiasts in Arizona and California, where he designed some important buildings, but no one I talked to there knew that he had left an architectural legacy in Marfa. It is as though he had two separate careers.

Dr. Beverly Brandt, professor of architectural history at Arizona State University, has told me that Knipe designed some of the earliest campus buildings there, one of which, Matthews Hall, built in 1918, is on the National Register of Historic Places. Brandt also told me that in 1918, Knipe played a major role in the design of the Southern Cotton Company's model company town, Litchfield Village, outside of Phoenix. The hotel he built there is now a popular golf resort, The Wigwam.

John Akers, curator of history at the Tempe Historical Society and another Knipe fan, filled in some biographical details for me. Knipe was born in Texas in 1878, went to Lafayette College in Pennsylvania, and called himself a structural engineer, rather than an architect. He built the Egyptian Revival Tempe National Bank, now being restored, in 1912 and became City Engineer of Tempe in 1913. Before coming to Arizona, Knipe worked for A. Prescott Fowell, one of the country's leading urban sanitary engineers.

Another Knipe enthusiast is Gwilym McGrew of Los Angeles who with his wife Peggy is restoring a six thousand square foot Spanish Colonial Revival ranch house in Woodland Hills, California, that Knipe designed in 1928 for millionaire John Show. The McGrews (whose e-mail address is "ProudCelts") and I have entered into a spirited correspondence about Knipe, and they have identified the tile he used on the façade of the Brite Building as being from the Claycroft Potteries in Los Angeles, an important art tile pottery in the 1920s. They also called my attention to a second large Spanish-style Knipe house in Los Angeles, the Orcutt Ranch House, built in 1926 for W. W. Orcutt, a pioneer California geologist and oilman. The Orcutt House is now a Los Angeles Historical Monument, owned by the city and open to the public.

The Orcutt House was built the same year that Knipe completed the First Christian Church in Marfa for Lucas Brite. Jane Brite White thinks that perhaps Knipe met her grandfather in Phoenix, because Brite owned a ranch near Phoenix and went there a good deal in the 1920s. However they met, Knipe's design for the First Christian Church was an eccentric expression of his own peculiar genius. It is the only church I have ever seen in which the sanctuary is not the most important room in the building. Knipe designed the church around an enormous octagonal community room with a stage on one of its sides and doors opening into the other spaces, including the sanctuary, on the other seven sides. The sanctuary is big—it will seat five hundred people—but the community room is clearly the most important room in the building. Perhaps it says something about the architect's feelings about the importance of community.

For some reason, Knipe gave up a promising career with wealthy patrons in Los Angeles to move to Marfa. Perhaps Brite promised him a steady string of commissions, and indeed built not only the Brite Building and the Marfa National Bank but also the little building that is now the Marfa Health Clinic. Or perhaps he was the first in an increasingly large crowd of cosmopolitan urbanites to reject big-city life and settle in Marfa. Whatever the reason, he gave Marfa a wonderful gift of distinguished buildings, and Marfans should be grateful to him.

January 19, 2006

✛ 21 ✛

THE DEAD MAN'S SPRINGS

LAST WEEK I found myself at a weirdly beautiful place with one of the more sinister-sounding names in the Big Bend, El Muerto Springs. It is not only sinister-sounding (the name means "the dead man"); it is isolated. I reached it by a dirt road that runs for twelve miles across two ranches north of Valentine, and when I was there, the only landmarks I could see were Sawtooth Mountain on the northern horizon and the Sierra Vieja to the south. There was a lot of cholla and catclaw in between. But during the thirty years that the stagecoaches traversed this part of Texas, from the early 1850s to the early 1880s, El Muerto Springs loomed large on travelers' mental maps. It was a stagecoach stop, a respite from hours of swaying and jouncing in a crowded coach, a place to have a meal and stretch your legs while the mule team that pulled the stage was changed.

I went there with Victoria Scism of Garland and a group of avocational archaeologists who, for the past several years, have been examining campsites on old trails in the Big Bend. El Muerto is hidden in a box canyon at the foot of some low hills, one of which bears the evocative name of Lonesome Lee. The spring flows out of the side of one of these hills, and the water drips down the wall of the canyon into a pool at its base, creating a slick black streak on the canyon wall. The pool is surrounded by tumbled boulders and oak trees. People have stopped here to refresh themselves for thousands of years. There are prehistoric petroglyphs on the canyon walls and grinding holes in the flat rocks. A more recent visitor left the date June 19, 1864, and an illegible name on a rock by the spring, and someone has built a picnic table and placed a rustic concrete bench under the largest oak tree.

The ruins of two stage stations are about three hundred feet from the spring, one built in 1859 by the Butterfield Overland Mail Company and the other built in the early 1870s by Benjamin Franklin Ficklin's Lightning Stage Line. Both lines had contracts to carry the mail from San Antonio to El Paso, and both built a line of stations at the waterholes along the road where herds of mules were kept to provide fresh relays for the teams that pulled the coaches. The two stations at El Muerto are typical. They were both high-walled stone corrals, about fifty feet on a side, with a strong wooden gate and two or three rooms built against the wall. One room served as a kitchen and dining room for the stage passengers, another as a bedroom for the two men who tended the station, and a third area was set aside for hay and fodder storage. The mule herd grazed under the watchful eye of the tender during the day and was shut into the corral at night.

The stations were in fact little forts, much like the French Foreign Legion forts that dotted the North African desert, but not as well manned. The tender and his assistant lived under constant threat of Indian attack; in fact, the first station at El Muerto, built in the early 1850s by mail contractor Henry Skillman, was so thoroughly destroyed by Apaches that its ruins have never been located. A rebuilt station, operated by Skillman's successor George H. Giddings, was burned to the ground by Apaches in January 1858, along with two coaches that were stopped there. The Butterfield station that replaced Giddings's was destroyed by Apaches when the route was abandoned during the Civil War. Ben Ficklin's replacement station was attacked several times in the 1870s, but the tenders blockaded themselves in the rock buildings and gave the mules to the Apaches.

Being a station tender was not only a dangerous job, it was a lonely one. The nearest station to the east of El Muerto was at Barrel Springs, fourteen miles away. To the west, it was thirty-two miles to the station at Van Horn Wells. The stagecoaches arrived once or twice a week and stayed for twenty minutes; the rest of the time the tenders had only their own company unless a party of travelers came along. During those long evenings, they had plenty of time to muse on the stories about Indian attacks that they gleefully passed on to stage passengers during their hurried meals. They might have thought about the all-night siege that station tender Light Townsend and his helpers underwent in 1859 at Van Horn Wells. The Apaches set the hay in the corral on fire, and twenty-six mules burned to death while Townsend and his men fired at the attackers through loopholes. The Indians knew Townsend by name, and one of them taunted him, calling in English "Luz Lightie, come out! We won't hurt you." Towards dawn, the roof caught fire and Townsend and his companions made a break for a nearby arroyo. The Apaches, satisfied with destroying the station and the mule herd, rode away, and the tenders started walking to Fort Davis.

One of the most repeated tales was about something that happened on the road between Van Horn Wells and Eagle Springs on a bitter cold January day in 1869. One of Ben Ficklin's agents, Henry Morrell, was riding on the box of an east-bound coach next to the driver when the mules shied at something in the road. The driver stopped and Morrell climbed down to discover that it was a battered human head. A few hundred feet down the road, they found an arm, and not far from that was the remnant of a body, badly gnawed by wolves. From some scraps of clothing, Morrell was able to identify it as that of James Bass, the driver of the coach that had left El Paso two days before his. The coach was a half-mile down the road, its upholstery stained with blood. In the road beside it was a carpet slipper, which was all that was left of the coach's single passenger, Jarvis Hubbell, a prominent El Pasoan who had been wearing it to ease a sore foot when he climbed into the coach in El Paso. His body was never found.

The stagecoaches stopped running on the San Antonio-El Paso road in 1882, when the railroad linking the two cities was completed. But last week, sitting at the picnic table by the spring and gazing east along the ruts that led back toward Barrel Springs and Fort Davis, I almost thought I could hear one coming.

November 29, 2007

✤ 22 ✤

JACK HOXIE AND HOLLYWOOD
IN FORT DAVIS

THE FILM fever that seized Marfa last summer, when two movies were being shot in town simultaneously, was old hat to the citizens of Fort Davis. It all happened there years ago, so long ago that most residents have forgotten about it or never knew that it had happened. But if you had been in Fort Davis in 1929 or 1930, you might have thought that you were only a few blocks from the corner of Hollywood and Vine. In May of 1929, the Hoxie Stockade and Motion Picture Company signed a lease on the old fort at Fort Davis, intending to turn the deteriorating buildings into a combination film studio and entertainment center.

Hollywood silent film star Jack Hoxie came to town that month with his leading lady, Dixie Starr (a seventeen-year-old ingénue whose real name was Dianne Hodges), and held a public meeting, at which he announced plans to add a fifty-by-eighty-foot swimming pool, an eighteen-hole golf course, a polo field, tennis courts, a dance pavilion, and a permanent film studio to the abandoned military post. The buildings on Officers' Row were to be restored to house the "movie colony," and a rodeo arena was to be built where performers would entertain crowds when they were not making movies. He offered the citizens of Fort Davis an opportunity to invest in this enterprise and sold numerous shares at $100 a pop.

Cecilia Thompson of Marfa, who grew up in Fort Davis and was nine years old when Hoxie held his meeting, remembers being impressed by Hoxie's flamboyant Western regalia and his

Buick roadster with cow horns mounted on the radiator. She told me that he threw a big picnic for the community under the cottonwoods at the fort, which her father would not let her attend because "movie people were not quite acceptable." She also remembers that Hoxie's party stayed at Rita Sproul's boarding house while they were in Fort Davis, and that when they left they did not pay their bill.

The year 1929 was not a good one to start a new business in Fort Davis or anywhere else in the United States. In October of that year the stock market crashed, plunging the country into the worst depression in its history. Hoxie's backers, a group of Oklahoma oilmen, turned out to be unable to meet their own obligations and could not provide Hoxie with the promised capital. Still, he plunged ahead. By March 1930, work had started on refurbishing the officers' quarters, and Hoxie announced a grand opening rodeo on March 23. His workers built a grandstand that would seat one thousand people, and on the big day, twice that number converged on Fort Davis from all over West Texas. They filled the grandstand and climbed over the ruined buildings, anxious to get a view of Hoxie, his horse Scout, his trained dog Bunk, and his Hollywood stars. What no one counted on was a West Texas dust storm, which made it impossible to see the arena and difficult for the riders to perform. The show was cut short, and shortly after that, Hoxie departed for a role in the Miller 101 Ranch Wild West Show. The performers went back to Hollywood, and the whole enterprise collapsed.

None of the local investors ever saw any return on their $100 shares, and as a result of that and the unpaid boarding house bill, Hoxie is remembered in Fort Davis as something of a fly-by-night, but in fact, he was a legitimate Western film star and his name is still familiar to silent film buffs. The 1920s were years when the real West and the reel West overlapped in Hollywood. Working cowboys from Western ranches, and not a few former outlaws, flocked to the film studios to get jobs as hard-riding extras and technical advisors. Oklahoma train robber Al Jennings, Marshal Bill Tilghman, Wyatt Earp, and Emmett Dalton all turned up in Hollywood. The corner of Cahuenga Avenue and Hollywood Boulevard was known as "the Waterhole" because cowboys would congregate there in boots, chaps, and Stetsons, waiting for hiring agents from studios that were filming westerns. Jack Hoxie was one of these cowboys.

Hoxie came up the hard way. He was born in Indian Territory in 1885. His father was killed shortly before his birth, and his mother married a horse trader and drifter named Scott Stone, who took the family to the Salmon River country of Idaho. Hoxie started cowboying there as a boy, worked for a while as a packer for the army, and in his mid-twenties, joined a wild west show called the Stanley Brothers Congress of Rough Riders, one of several hundred knock-offs of Buffalo Bill's Wild West that toured the country in those years. He honed his riding and roping skills under the tutelage of fellow Stanley Brothers performer Hoot Gibson.

Hoxie arrived at the Waterhole in 1913, and by 1919 he had been cast in thirty-five films. He added trick shooting to his riding and roping skills, and his trademark became the crossdraw, in which his right hand reached for the pistol on his left hip and his left hand for the one on his right hip. He and his Appaloosa horse Scout hit pay dirt in 1919, when he was cast as the lead in a fifteen-part serial called *Lightning Bryce*. By the mid-1920s, he was one of the ten top-drawing Western stars in the nation, right up there with Hoot Gibson, Art Acord, and Harry Carey. His half-brother Al Stone joined him in Hollywood and often played his sidekick under the name Al Hoxie. In 1926, Jack Hoxie portrayed a memorable Buffalo Bill Cody in Universal Pictures' *The Last Frontier*, alongside young William Boyd, who in the 1950s thrilled a new generation of fans as television's Hopalong Cassidy.

Hoxie had just one problem. His fancy riding, roping, and shooting were perfect for action-packed silent films, but he was unable to memorize lines, and when movies started talking, he was out. He tried to make a comeback in Hollywood after the Fort Davis venture, and made six short sound films in 1933, but after that, his career was limited to circuses and Wild West shows. He made his last tour with the Bill Tatum Circus in 1959 and died of leukemia in 1965. As far as I know, he never came back to Fort Davis, and he never paid his bill at Rita Sproul's boarding house.

August 9, 2007

✣ 23 ✣

STANLEY MARCUS, CIVILIZED TEXAN

THE HALL OF STATE in Dallas is a monumental and lavishly decorated art deco building at Fair Park, constructed to house the State of Texas's history exhibit at the 1936 Texas Centennial Exposition. It is now the home of the Dallas Historical Society. Against the wall of its semi-circular entrance hall are life-size bronze statues by Pompeo Coppini of six Texas heroes: Stephen F. Austin, Sam Houston, Mirabeau B. Lamar, William B. Travis, James W. Fannin, and Thomas Jefferson Rusk. Several years ago, a newly appointed director of the Dallas Historical Society solicited the names of six twentieth-century Texas heroes to supplement these nineteenth-century figures. I sent in my suggestions, a list of twentieth-century statesmen (and stateswomen) who I thought were worthy successors to these bronze giants. But on reflection, I realized that I had omitted my favorite twentieth-century Texan, a man who never held public office—Stanley Marcus.

Marcus, who died in 2002 at the age of ninety-six, is best known to Texans as the president of the Dallas department store that his family founded in 1914—Neiman-Marcus. But in addition to being a merchant and taste-setter, he was the most civilized Texan of his day, a bibliophile, art collector, oenophile, and gourmet at a time when most of the world thought of Texans as loud, obnoxious, super-rich clods. Stanley Marcus was as much at home on the Champs-Élysées as he was on Main Street in Dallas, and he did his best to educate his customers to move in the wider world with the same ease that he did.

My first introduction to Paris and London came from the French and British Fortnights that Marcus produced at Neiman's in 1957 and 1958. The fortnights were not limited to the store. For the French Fortnight, the Dallas Museum of Fine Arts did a special exhibit of Toulouse-Lautrec paintings from the Musée d'Albi, and the artist Bernard Buffet gave a lecture. There was a French tapestry exhibit at the Dallas Municipal Auditorium. Best of all, the Zodiac Room served French pastries for two weeks. For the British Fortnight the next year, the Old Vic came to Dallas for a week and a London bobby directed traffic in front of the store. For a culture-hungry teenager living in Fort Worth, it was paradise just thirty miles away.

What distinguished Marcus from other Texas merchant princes of the 1950s and '60s was that he had a genuine desire to make Texas a less provincial place. Speaking about the history of retailing, he once told the *New York Times* that "it was the department store that helped people get away from provincialism." He not only supported Dallas's art museum, library, and symphony, but he chaired the Dallas World Affairs Council at a time when many Dallasites, encouraged by the right-wing editorials of the *Dallas Morning News*, thought that the United Nations was part of a Communist plot. Most of Neiman-Marcus's customers were fairly conservative Republicans, and when Marcus came out for John Kennedy in 1960, some of them closed their charge accounts. But, as he says in his book, *Minding the Store* (University of North Texas Press, 1997), they continued to shop at the store; they just paid cash.

I was present at the October 1963 speech by Adlai Stevenson in the Dallas Municipal Auditorium at which Stanley Marcus introduced Stevenson to an audience that was stacked with John Birchers and worse, who were intent on preventing him from speaking. When the boos and hisses and catcalls started, Marcus shouldered a bewildered Stevenson away from the podium and, in a steely voice, asked for order. A well-dressed and beautifully-coifed blonde in the audience stood up and started to reply and Marcus pointed the gavel at her and said, "You sit down and shut up." That probably cost him a customer or two, but it brought order for a few minutes, even though the meeting later deteriorated into a shoving match during which both Marcus and Stevenson were spit upon and hit with a picket sign. Marcus later asked Lyndon B. Johnson to try to dissuade John Kennedy from coming to Dallas. After the assassination, he took out a full-page ad in both Dallas papers urging Dallasites to "be tolerant of different points of view" and to "reject the spirit of absolutism from which our community has suffered." I think his efforts, combined with the shock of the assassination, had an effect; Dallas became a much more tolerant city in the 1970s and '80s.

Marcus was a consummate merchant. He knew that his customers wanted something special from him, something they could not buy anywhere else but Neiman's. In the early 1960s, he started putting discreet little labels on some merchandise that said, "Made in Spain Especially for Neiman-Marcus" or "Made in Switzerland Especially for Neiman-Marcus." I had a college classmate, a vivacious woman with a bubbling sense of humor, who took a job at the stationery counter of Neiman's Fort Worth store. Among the merchandise in her department were some little faux-antique wooden boxes, painted white with gold trim. My friend made a sign, which she propped on the counter beside them that said, "Made in Sixteenth-Century Florence Especially for Neiman-Marcus." The second day that it was up, Mr. Stanley, as everyone who worked at the store called him, came by on one of his regular perambulations around the sales floor. He stopped, read the sign, looked at my friend, and said, "Young lady, I'd like to see you in my office at three o'clock." My friend was sure that she had lost her job, but when she got to Mr. Stanley's office, he gave her a cup of coffee, complimented her on her sense of humor, and told her he had ordered labels with her legend on them for the boxes.

March 6, 2008

II. TEXAS FAMILY

24

FAMILY SAGAS

ONE OF THE SESSIONS I went to at the Texas State Historical Association's meeting in Austin last month was devoted to the folkloristic notion of the family saga, an idea developed by the University of Texas English professor Mody Boatright in the late 1950s. Boatright was a West Texan who had spent a lot of time as a boy sitting on front porches listening to his elders tell family stories, and as an adult, he pondered what these stories meant. The speakers all explained that Boatright's term "saga" did not mean a long, coherent narrative, as in the Norse sagas, but rather a loosely-knit group of stories about family members, preserved and passed on by their descendants. Each speaker then told some stories that had been passed on in their families and speculated a little about why the stories had been preserved and what they meant.

I left the session thinking about some of the stories that have been preserved in my family, and what they might mean. My grandmother Taylor, who lived with us when I was growing up, was a great one for stories. One time when she was in her eighties, we had cherries with dinner, and she informed the table that one could get drunk eating wild cherries. When my father asked her to explain, she said that once when she was about ten, her two older brothers went into town on a Saturday and came home just as drunk as they could be. When their father asked them what was the matter with them, they replied, "Why, Papa, we've been eating wild cherries." What this story meant was that her brothers may not have fooled their father, but they had fooled their little sister for seventy years.

My grandmother's father was an ex-Confederate soldier who came to Texas after the Civil War and tried to make a living as a freighter. She had a whole cycle of stories about him which she repeated often. They were all intended to show what an admirable person he was, emphasizing his courage in the face of adversity, his gentle nature, and his abhorrence of alcohol. However, there was one story that only emerged long after my grandmother's death. I was at a family funeral, and one of my cousins was talking about how stubborn my grandmother had been. "She must have gotten that from her father," my cousin said. "All the Borders were stubborn." When I asked what she meant, she told a story that she had heard from her mother, my grandmother's little sister. According to her, my great-grandfather was trying to get one of his wagons across the creek at Round Rock when the axle hung fast on a rock. He was urging the oxen forward in the time-honored method of teamsters, turning the air blue with strong language, when he heard a voice on the bluff above him. It was the Methodist preacher, who said, "Mr. Border, if you will stop cursing, my son John and I will come down and help you move your wagon."

"You and your son John can go to hell," my great-grandfather replied. "I got this wagon on this damned rock by myself and I will damn well get it off by myself." I think what this meant was that my grandmother did not like stories that involved profanity and showed disrespect for the clergy. But it also meant that I suddenly acquired a great deal more respect for my great-grandfather.

My mother never talked very much about her side of the family while my father was alive, but when she was in her early nineties, she started telling me her family stories. One evening after dinner, she told me about her Aunt Coonie, whom I remembered as a quiet old lady who ran a tourist home in Asheville, North Carolina. According to my mother, Aunt Coonie had eloped when she was sixteen with a cowboy who worked on a neighboring ranch in Wise County. Her father, my mother's grandfather, was furious and had the marriage annulled, and he kept a pretty close watch on Aunt Coonie for the next few years. But when she was in her early twenties, in the 1920s, she fell in love with a handsome and dashing young man she met at a Colorado summer resort. He parted his hair in the middle, wore good suits, drove a Pierce-Arrow roadster, and sold stocks and bonds from an office in Denver. The whole family was delighted when they got married, and my mother thought her new Uncle Wallace was the bee's knees. Then it developed that Uncle Wallace mostly sold stock in mines that didn't exist, and a family conclave was held at which it was strongly suggested to Uncle Wallace that he take a job that Aunt Coonie's sister, who was a prominent Denver businesswoman, had found for him selling typewriters in Kansas City. This sounded like a solution, but Uncle Wallace no sooner got set up in the typewriter business than he was caught with his hand in the till and took a pistol and blew his brains out. Aunt Coonie wired her oldest brother, who went to Kansas City and sent the rest of the family a series of telegrams that read, "Wallace very sick," "Wallace in hospital," "Wallace died yesterday; no need to come to funeral." My mother said it was years before she learned what actually happened.

What does this family story mean? Besides being a perfect gloss on America in the 1920s, I think it means that Aunt Coonie was a much more interesting person than I realized when I was growing up, and I wish I had spent more time with her.

April 6, 2006

25

MY GRANDMOTHER TAYLOR

MY GRANDMOTHER Taylor was a woman of strong character and certain unshakable convictions. Her character was formed early in life. She was born in 1877 in Round Rock, Texas. Her father was a former Confederate soldier who came to Texas after the war and started a freight business, hauling goods in ox wagons from railheads to West Texas; her mother was the daughter of a Louisiana cotton planter who, I think, pined for her former life. She died when my grandmother was twelve, and her husband sold his freight wagons and became a cotton farmer so that he could stay home and look after his children. He moved from place to place, always hoping for a better crop next year. One of the farms they lived on was next to a plantation worked by convicts; he gave my grandmother a conch shell with a hole drilled in the pointed end and told her that if anyone approached the house while he was away to blow on it and he would hear it and come in from the fields. At times they were desperately poor. Once when I was in my teens, my grandmother told me that I did not know how lucky I was to be able to eat meat every day. When she was a little girl, she said, her family had meat only on Sundays; the rest of the week it was beans and cornbread.

The convictions that she held were not acquired in school, because her education had ended with the fifth grade. They were derived from the folk wisdom of the late nineteenth-century rural South, and she held to them tenaciously through a good part of the twentieth century.

She grew up in farmhouses without electricity, and she was

convinced that electric appliances had malign powers. She knew without a doubt that telephones had the ability to transmit lightning into houses, and that the best way to prevent this was to break the circuit by taking the receiver off the hook. Consequently, during all the years that she lived with us, no one could ever call our house during a storm, because my grandmother would have gone from room to room when it started, taking the telephone receivers out of their cradles. She also knew that if you rode on an electric streetcar, your watch would stop, and when we lived in Washington, DC at the end of World War II, she avoided streetcar trips like the plague, walking blocks out of her way to ride the bus instead. My father would point out to her that he took a streetcar to his office and back every day and it had no effect at all on his wristwatch. She would answer that when Austin first got electric streetcars in 1891, her brother got on one and his watch stopped as soon as he took his seat, and that was that.

She was born the year that Reconstruction in the South ended, and she grew up listening to her father and his friends recount their adventures as Confederate soldiers. Her father belonged to a cavalry unit that had simply disbanded at the end of the war; the captain told his men to take their horses and get home as best they could. Consequently, he had never formally surrendered to the Union Army. My grandmother attached great significance to this fact and whenever she spoke of her father, no matter what the context, she would always add, "And he never surrendered!" When we were living in the Philippines in the early 1950s, my grandmother managed to lose her American passport, and she had to go to the American embassy in Manila to apply for a new one. This was at the height of the Joe McCarthy-inspired Red Scare, and applicants for passports had to answer a long list of questions designed to ascertain their loyalty to the United States. The very first question on the list was, "Has any member of your family ever borne arms against the government of the United

States?" My grandmother enthusiastically answered, "Yes! And he never surrendered!" The Filipino clerk who was taking down her answers excused himself, wide-eyed, and fortunately found an embassy officer who knew about old Southern ladies and told him, "Don't worry, that's not the war we're concerned about."

These memories of my grandmother were evoked recently by an elderly lady tourist who walked into the barracks at Fort Davis National Historic Site, where I serve occasionally as a volunteer guide. She went straight to the portrait of Abraham Lincoln that hangs over the door, peered at it, and said, "My grandfather was a cousin of Jefferson Davis and he looked just like that—the same hollow cheeks." I didn't say a word, but I remembered that one of my grandmother's most unshakable convictions was that Jefferson Davis and Abraham Lincoln were half-brothers, Lincoln being the illegitimate son of Davis's father Samuel Emory Davis and Nancy Hanks. I can still remember the stunned silence when my grandmother casually stated this at one of my parents' dinner parties, as if it were a fact of American history known to every school child. My father asked her where she had learned that and she said, "Why, my father told me. You only have to look at their pictures to see that they were related—the same hollow cheeks."

For years I assumed that this was just a folktale, but then I heard the same story from the Houston philanthropist Ima Hogg, the daughter of Texas governor James Stephen Hogg, who told me that she had heard it as a child from a political friend of her father's named Francis Lubbock. Lubbock had been an aide to Jefferson Davis at the end of the war and had been with him when he was captured by Union troops in Georgia in May of 1865. Miss Hogg said that Lubbock told her father that Davis himself believed the story, and had told Lubbock that Abraham Lincoln had been sent by God to punish him (Davis) for his father's sin. My grandmother's father had been part of the cavalry escort that accompanied Davis and his party during their flight from Richmond and was with them to the end. It is just possible that he heard the story from Davis, or picked it up from someone who had, in the way that stories filter through an army. At any rate, perhaps all of my grandmother's convictions were not just folk wisdom. That one may have come straight from the horse's mouth.

August 30, 2007

✤ 26 ✤

UNCLE WILL

I N M O S T Western European cultures there is a special relationship between uncles and nephews. Fathers discipline sons and set their feet on the path to manhood, but uncles ease their nephews' way along that path by teaching them things that it would be inappropriate for fathers to address. Usually these things have to do with alcohol, tobacco, and sex, but my favorite uncle, my Uncle Will, died when I was eight, so he did not have an opportunity to broach these subjects. Instead, he taught me how to tie my shoelaces, how to use a lariat, and how to drive a team of mules.

Uncle Will was my grandmother Taylor's older brother. He was born in 1875 in a double-pen log house in Milam County, Texas, but he spent most of his life in Hungerford, Texas, a town of two hundred people in Wharton County, where he raised cattle and grew cotton, and that was where I knew him.

Uncle Will was a very short man with big ears, an outrageous sense of humor, and a quick temper. He lived with his wife, my Aunt Jenny, in a rambling frame house facing the railroad tracks that ran through Hungerford. Across the street was the Farmers' Coop Cotton Gin, and across the tracks were the post office, the general store, the café, and the J. D. Hudgins Ranch office, where his sister-in-law, my Aunt Eola, presided over the cattle registry books. That was the world in which my Uncle Will let me follow him around when we visited him. Once when I was five, he took me to the café for lunch and told the waitress, "This boy lives in Washington, DC, and he would like a panther steak covered with skunk sauce." When the meal came, I happily scarfed down a chicken-fried steak drenched in cream gravy, the first one I had ever tasted, thinking about what my parents would say when I told them I had eaten panther meat for lunch. I decided I wouldn't mention the sauce.

It was in that same café that a traveling salesman overheard Uncle Will and another man having a heated discussion in an adjacent booth. Voices were raised, threats were exchanged. The salesman slipped to the pay phone and called the sheriff. "I'm out here in Hungerford, and there are two men here in the café who are awful mad at each other. I think there might be a killing unless you get out here quick."

"Is one of them a little short fellow with big ears?" the sheriff asked. When the salesman said he was, the sheriff said, "Leave 'em alone. That's Will Border and if he got killed it would be the best thing that ever happened to Wharton County."

Actually, the sheriff, Buckshot Lane, was a good friend of Uncle Will's and knew he was all bark and no bite. Besides, Uncle Will and Sheriff Lane shared a guilty secret: they had burned a bridge together. For years, a narrow wooden bridge at Kendleton, on the main road between Houston and Wharton, had been the cause of automobile accidents. In spite of repeated requests from the county commissioners, the state highway department refused to widen the bridge. One night in 1936, after a particularly grue-some wreck, Uncle Will, Buckshot Lane, and several other men drove a gasoline tank truck to the bridge, opened the valve, drove the truck across the bridge, and then lit a match to the gasoline-soaked timbers. Whenever I asked Uncle Will to tell me about it, he would grin and say, "Well, I wasn't there, but I remember what it looked like," and then describe the flames leaping across the bridge.

In 1946, Uncle Will and Aunt Jenny drove from Texas to Washington, DC, to visit us. I was all excited about their coming, and told all my playmates that my uncle was a real cowboy and wore boots, which was all I had ever seen him in. I was mortified when he got out of his car wearing a suit and vest and old-fashioned high-top shoes. He had dressed up for his first trip to the East. He redeemed himself a few days later, however, when he visited the neighborhood barber shop and came back to report with a straight face that his beard was so tough that the barber had broken three straight razors trying to shave him.

It was during that visit that Uncle Will taught me to tie my shoes. I had just turned six, and I was completely baffled by the intricacies of bow knots. My parents were absolutely no help. Uncle Will took the situation in as soon as he arrived and saw my flapping shoelaces. The next morning, he took me out to the back steps, had me put a foot up on one, knelt down behind me, and guided my fingers through the knot-tying motions. I had it down pat in three minutes. Then for good measure, he found a piece of clothesline and showed me how to tie the knot that would turn it into a lariat. I spent hours in my bedroom practicing the toss he had shown me on my bedpost, and then I moved on to our cat, and then to the neighbors' dogs. At that point, my mother strongly suggested that I put the lariat away until we went to Texas the next summer.

The following summer, when I was seven, Uncle Will taught me how to drive a team of mules. He had an old wagon and a pair of mules in a barn behind his house, and one morning he hitched the mules to the wagon, put me up on the seat with him, and gave me the reins. He stood up behind me in the wagon bed, showed me how to thread the reins through my fingers, and then put his hands over mine as the mules pulled the wagon around the barnyard. We did this every morning all summer long, eventually extending the range of our drives to the post office across the tracks. Years later, when I was an adult running a farm museum and had occasion to drive a team of mules, I discovered that the reins fit naturally between my fingers and that I knew exactly what to do with them. Thanks to Uncle Will, I am one of the few urban-raised children of my generation who knows how to handle a team of mules.

June 28, 2007

✣ 27 ✣

AUNT BESSIE

WHENEVER my cousins from Wharton County and I get together, we invariably start telling stories about Aunt Bessie. Aunt Bessie was actually my great-aunt, my grandmother's little sister, and she lived most of her life on a ranch outside of Hungerford, Texas. Aunt Bessie had inherited some oil and gas income from her husband, who died when she was still a relatively young woman, and she was a sort of Auntie Mame to her grandchildren and her grandnieces and grandnephews.

Aunt Bessie was born in 1882, so by the time I was old enough to form an impression of her, she was in her sixties. She was short and plump, and her round blue eyes gave her an uncanny resemblance to the aging Queen Victoria. She was far from Victorian, however. She loved parties and she loved trips, and she flung herself enthusiastically into both. She once decided that her grandchildren needed to see the Calgary Stampede, and she put them in her car and headed to Canada without any luggage and without bothering to tell their parents where they were going. Instead, she called them from Dallas when she stopped at Neiman-Marcus to buy clothes and other necessities for the trip. When she got to Calgary, she went to the Stampede offices and said, "I'm Mrs. Joel Hudgins from Hungerford, Texas, and I'd like tickets for myself and my grandchildren for the rodeo." They were so impressed by her demeanor that they gave her complimentary box seats.

Aunt Bessie bought a new Cadillac every other year and she loved to drive. She did not like to be confined to roads and she frequently took off across pastures and old rice fields to show her passengers something of interest, which is one reason she needed a new car every two years. She was also blissfully unaware of speed limits and was frequently stopped by highway patrolmen. I recall one of her narratives of such an encounter.

"I was on the Boling Highway and was doing about eighty and I saw this red light flashing behind me, so I pulled over on the shoulder and looked in the rear view mirror and I saw this young man in a uniform get out of his car. Well, I locked the car doors and I took off my watch and my rings and I locked them in the glove compartment and then I rolled down my window and said, 'Young man, whatever do you want?'"

She usually got away with a warning ticket. Toward the end of her life, she hired a young man named Fred Lara to drive for her, and he bravely followed her instructions to drive across pastures and into cotton fields.

I spent the summer that I was fifteen at Aunt Bessie's ranch, getting to know my cousins and absorbing Aunt Bessie's stories about Wharton County's past. When I grew older, I realized that some of those stories were tinged with a romanticism that may have come from having seen *Gone With the Wind* too many times. Aunt Bessie owned several small cotton farms which she referred to as her "plantations," although none of them was larger than two or three hundred acres, and she was fond of saying things like, "I was driving from my upper plantation to my lower plantation when a tire blew out." One evening we were sitting on the porch with my grandmother and my great-uncles, and Aunt Bessie was telling me that their mother's father had once been wounded in a duel. One of her brothers said, "Now, Bess, you know it wasn't a duel. He accused a neighbor of stealing his pigs and the man lay for him with a shotgun and shot him in the arm."

A duel figured in another of her stories. There was a big tumble down house not far from her ranch that was known as the Old Hood Place. I asked Aunt Bessie about it one day and she told me that Mr. Hood had been a very wealthy planter who had killed a man in a duel and had to leave the state. Since the house dated from the 1850s, I assumed that the duel had taken place sometime before the Civil War. It was not until I read Horton Foote's account of his youth in Wharton, *Farewell,* that I learned what had actually happened. Sometime in the 1930s, the bank in Wharton foreclosed on a note from Mr. Hood and Hood walked into the bank and shot the president dead—hardly a duel.

Aunt Bessie had a somewhat romantic view of her own past, too. After her husband's death she was courted by several men who saw her as an attractive widow with an attractive fortune, and on at least one occasion her brothers felt constrained to intervene before things went too far. "One of my suitors," she told me wistfully, "was the richest oil man in Houston, and he gave me an apple-green Pierce-Arrow convertible, but my brothers would not let me accept it, and it sat in a crate at the Hungerford railroad station until it was washed away in a flood."

One of the joys of staying at Aunt Bessie's big ranch house was that you never knew who would be at the breakfast table. Her in-laws, who owned a ranch adjacent to hers, sold Brahma bulls to ranchers all over the world, and when cattle buyers came, Aunt Bessie always put them up. The summer that I stayed with her, I met ranchers from Nicaragua, Brazil, Australia, and South Africa. One morning I got up very early and as I went out the front door, I was surprised to see Aunt Bessie sitting on the sofa in the living room smiling benignly at two young men who were kneeling in front of her, open Bibles in their hands. They were not at breakfast and when I asked Aunt Bessie who they were she said, "You know, those young men weren't cattle buyers at all. They were Jehovah's Witnesses." They had arrived at the ranch late in the evening and Aunt Bessie, without inquiring what they wanted, had shown them to empty bedrooms and said she would see them in the morning.

I still have the letter of introduction that Aunt Bessie wrote for me when I went off to graduate school in New York. It says, "This will introduce my nephew Lonn Wood Taylor of Fort Worth. Any courtesy shown will be appreciated by me. Mrs. Joel Hudgins, Hungerford, Texas." Aunt Bessie didn't know anybody in New York, but she was pretty sure that people there knew who she was.

July 31, 2008

✤ 28 ✤

MY DEAD GRANDFATHER

WHENEVER I hear someone talk about grandfathers I feel deprived because both of mine died before I was born. It is my grandfather Taylor that I most regret not having known because he was an adventurer. My grandfather Wood was a small-town druggist and a good man, I am sure—at least my mother thought so—but my grandfather Taylor, whose name was the same as mine, was a peace officer, a soldier, and something of a scamp. He died when my father was nineteen, so all I know of him is from my father's memories and my grandmother's somewhat guarded comments. From those, I have gathered that he was a hard man for a woman to live with but an easy man for a boy to love.

He was born in 1865 in Farmersville, Texas, north of Dallas, and grew up in McKinney, where his father owned a grocery store. As a young man, he learned the saddlemaker's trade. I have his shaving mug, a ceramic mug that depicts a man working at a saddlemaker's stitching horse above his name in gilt Gothic letters. When he finished his apprenticeship, he went to work for his brother-in-law, who owned a string of trading posts across the Red River in the Choctaw and Cherokee Nations. He made saddles and harnesses for those stores, but he also spent a lot of time running foot races with the local boys. He was fleet-footed, and his brother-in-law won a good deal of money by moving him from town to town and placing bets on him in places where he was not known.

Sometime in the 1890s, he got bored with store work, took a number of odd jobs, and eventually signed on as a Deputy US Marshal for the federal court in Fort Smith, Arkansas, which had jurisdiction over parts of the Indian Territory. For the next few years, he tracked murderers, thieves, and all sorts of petty criminals across the Indian Nations, arrested them, and brought them to justice in Fort Smith. My grandfather later told my father that the worst people in the United States ended up in Indian Territory and that it was his job to chase them down. He particularly hated going into the Winding Stair Mountains, which he said was the thickest nest of thieves in North America.

As a boy, I had visions of my grandfather chasing outlaws on horseback, Lone Ranger style, but my father told me he was a cautious and prudent man. He always traveled by buggy, and when he found his man, he would disarm him, handcuff him beside him on the seat, and drive him to Fort Smith. At night, he would unhitch his horse, build a campfire, feed his prisoner, lay out a bedroll for him, and handcuff him to the buggy wheel. Then he would ride the horse to a spot a mile or so away and make his own camp for the night. If his prisoner managed to get loose, my grandfather didn't want to be found, but he never lost a prisoner.

When the Spanish-American War came along, he joined a regular army regiment, the Twenty-Third Infantry, as a thirty-three-year-old private. He did not join a volunteer regiment because, he told my father, if he was going to be shot at on a regular basis, he wanted to be with people who knew what they were doing. He went to the Philippine Islands, helped to capture Manila from the Spanish, fought against the *insurrectos*, and took his discharge two years later on the island of Jolo. He came back to Texas, married my grandmother, and spent the rest of his life running a series of unsuccessful grocery stores and working for a Fort Worth printing company. My grandmother was always embarrassed to show me his elaborately engraved discharge certificate because it said that his occupation before joining the army was "bartender." She claimed that he had told the enlisting officer that as a joke, but I am not so sure.

My grandfather was not a good businessman. He was a frontiersman whom the frontier passed by. As my father once put it to me, he was not a successful man, judged by the credo of his times, but he was a successful father. After he lost his last grocery store by being too generous with credit, he got a job in a flour mill, but on Christmas Day of 1911, he caught his leg in some mill machinery and nearly lost it, and from then until his death in 1922, he had a job cleaning lithograph plates at the Stafford-Lowden Printing Company, a job he could perform sitting down.

He had one chance to become a rich man. During the Mexican Revolution, one of the revolutionary generals who was in exile in Texas placed an order with Stafford-Lowden for millions of pesos worth of currency, which he planned to put into circulation as soon as he returned to power. My grandfather and several of the printers went down to the shop at night and ran off several million extra pesos, planning to move to Mexico and live like kings when the general's revolution was successful. Unfortunately it was not successful, and the uncut sheets of worthless pesos never left Fort Worth.

I think that he was a kind man. He was an excellent rifle shot, and when his regiment was in camp in San Francisco, waiting to go to the Philippines, he participated in the regimental shooting match. He won his squad match, and then his company match, and finally there was only one man left in the regiment with a score as high as his, and they were scheduled to shoot against each other for the regimental championship. However, the regiment was suddenly ordered to embark for the Philippines and the final match never came off. My grandfather thought that his rival looked familiar, and when his troop ship got to Manila, he got into his footlocker and went through his old book of wanted posters. He realized that his would-be opponent was a criminal that he had tracked back in Indian Territory and never caught up with. And so, he told my father, he never found out what would have happened if he had found him. The point of the story is that the man had enlisted in the army under an assumed name, and he took his discharge before my grandfather. He opened a small business in Manila and prospered. My grandfather thought he deserved a second chance and so he never revealed his true identity.

July 14, 2005

✢ 29 ✢

FORT WORTH BARS

ERNEST HEMINGWAY has a lot to answer for. He may have been the best American writer of his time, but he had a baneful influence on the health and deportment of a whole generation of young men who grew up wanting to be writers in the 1950s. I was one of those young men, and my aspiring-writer friends and I were convinced from reading Hemingway that if we wanted to write about life, we had first to experience it. Experiencing life meant hanging around bars and rubbing shoulders with "real" people, real people being people who were not our parents' friends or our professors, but the down-and-outers and boozers that Hemingway's characters associated with in the alleys behind Les Halles or the bars of Montmartre. Unfortunately, my friends and I were not growing up in Paris but in Fort Worth, Texas. Nevertheless, we sought out authenticity and gritty reality in whatever bars and honky-tonks we could brazen our underage selves into, always keeping an eye on the door for the Liquor Control Board agent who might appear to check IDs.

Of course, there was the standard off-campus college bar, a dive on Berry Street called Duke's, but we had to share Duke's with fraternity boys and their girlfriends and the occasional jock who was breaking training. Duke's did have the attraction of having an owner who used to hint vaguely of having underworld connections, and it had a resident authentic character, an older man called Cowboy who had allegedly once been arrested for riding a horse down Berry Street while inebriated, but in general it was too tame for most of us, and we eventually shifted our after-class drinking activities to a group of bars downtown along Lower Main Street.

Lower Main Street was the lineal descendant of a neighborhood that in the 1880s was called Hell's Half Acre, a conglomeration of saloons and bawdy houses that made Fort Worth notorious among Western towns. By the late 1950s it had come to resemble the Bowery more than Dodge City, but some of its denizens still carried concealed weapons. Our favorite spot there was a place called Corita's Ice Man's Lounge, whose elderly patrons sat around on upended Coca-Cola cases drinking beer, as the chairs and tables had disappeared years ago. The entertainment at Corita's was a fiddler named Junior Moody, who claimed to have been the World's Champion Fiddler in 1928 and who could still, when reasonably sober, play a mean version of "Leather Britches." His specialty, however, was what he called his "trick fiddle," which involved holding both the fiddle and bow behind his back and playing "The Yellow Rose of Texas." For a while there was a motorcycle that stood on its kickstand in the middle of Corita's. A patron had ridden into the bar on it one night and when the police came to remove him, the motorcycle had remained behind. When Junior really hit his stride, someone would jump on the motorcycle and rev up the engine in time with his fiddle.

If we got bored at Corita's, we could always go down the street to the Do or Don't Lounge, which did not offer live music but had a jukebox that dated from the late 1930s. The patrons there, however, were a little younger and occasionally more dangerous than the crowd at Corita's. One night I got up from a table at the Do or Don't to visit the men's room. As I started across the dance floor, I felt a tug on my sleeve and heard a voice saying, "Son, I don't believe I'd step across there just now." I looked up and realized that I was about to walk in front of a bartender who was pointing a revolver at a customer and ordering him to leave. I left first.

In my senior year of college, I found what I thought was the ultimate honky-tonk. It was an old frame building on Hemphill Street called the 1311 Club. I dropped in there one afternoon and found an elderly white man playing the most low-down blues I had ever heard on the bar piano and about half a dozen harmless-looking old geezers in their seventies and eighties listening to him. I soon discovered that he was there every afternoon, and my friends and I became regular afternoon patrons. One day I heard that he was going to play there the following Friday night, and I determined to bring a date with me to hear him, in spite of the fact that I had been told that the place was pretty rough at night. For some reason we didn't go that Friday night, and the next morning I picked up the *Fort Worth Press* to see a picture of the barmaid at the 1311 being led out of the front door by the police, her dress covered with blood. The accompanying story said that someone had walked in the door, pulled out a pistol, and started shooting at the barmaid. She had ducked under the bar, picked up what the paper described as the "bar pistol," a .45 automatic, and started shooting back. The lights went out, her assailant fell dead across the bar, and an autopsy showed that he had been shot in the back by someone on the other side of the room. When the police showed up, they took a pistol off each of the remaining nine customers. It seemed that an entirely different group of people went in there at night.

One of our crowd did write a novel, and another published some fine short stories, several of which were set in bars, so maybe our youthful search for real life paid off for some of us. Looking back, I'm just glad I survived.

April 27, 2006

BEATNIKS ON CAMP BOWIE
BOULEVARD

M Y FRIEND Dink Starns called me from Fort Worth the other day to remind me that the fiftieth anniversary of the opening of the Black Beret was coming up on March 29. No ceremony is planned and no historical marker will be unveiled, but the Black Beret deserves at least a footnote in the cultural history of Texas, and this essay will be that footnote. The Black Beret was the coffee house that Starns and his business partner Louis Page operated in Fort Worth in 1959 and 1960, and during its short life, it provided a tantalizing reflection of Greenwich Village to culture-hungry West Texans.

In the spring and summer of 1959, a coffee house craze swept the entire United States and coffee houses modeled on New York's Le Figaro and San Francisco's Vesuvio opened in every major city and many small towns. At one point that summer there were half a dozen in Fort Worth alone. They all served espresso and cappucino, or at least reasonable facsimiles thereof; they all featured someone reciting poetry to the thud of a pair of bongo drums or a young woman in a black body stocking who sat on a stool and strummed a guitar; and they all offered a sense of adventure and possibility to the young people who gathered in them every night and pretended that they were in North Beach or Greenwich Village. In fact, they were frequently referred to not just as "coffee houses" but as "Greenwich Village coffee houses."

The Black Beret was the first to open in Fort Worth and it was by far the classiest. Starns and Page employed waiters and they actually owned an espresso machine from Italy, a big bulbous brass dome surmounted by a brass eagle which made a satisfying hissing noise punctuated by bursts of steam, like a locomotive at rest. They served a variety of coffees and pastries, and young people would gather there to play chess, talk, read, and listen to music. People would drive from Denton, Abilene, and even Lubbock to partake of the Bohemian atmosphere. On Friday and Saturday night there was a trio with an accordion, a family band of stranded Belgians who wore black berets and played "Tzana, Tzana" and "La Vie en Rose." The coffee house was next to an art supply shop on Camp Bowie Boulevard, not far from the Fort Worth Art Center and the Carlin Gallery. It was as close as you could get to an artsy neighborhood in Fort Worth in 1959.

Starns and Page were the closest thing to sophisticated men of the world that Fort Worth could produce, at least in the eyes of the nineteen-year-old college sophomore that I was then. They were both bachelors in their late twenties; they both drove black Mercedes-Benz sedans purchased on trips to Europe; and they shared a house on Lake Worth to which favored customers were sometimes invited after the close of business to sip single-malt Scotch, listen to jazz records, and talk about life. Sometimes beautiful women were present who showed every intention of staying there all night.

Some of the customers were quite picturesque. There was a bearded man in his late thirties known as Colonel, who wore a bush jacket and always managed to give the impression, without actually saying so, that his rank derived from adventures as a soldier of fortune in Africa. I later learned that he was actually a bricklayer from Fort Worth's Northside, and that whatever African experience he had was in construction work. Another habitué was an auto mechanic whose rather startling costume consisted of a short-sleeved khaki shirt and British army shorts worn over a suit of long underwear, and who would recite verses by Allen Ginsberg and Lawrence Ferlinghetti in a menacing growl.

Of course the Black Beret soon had imitators. The best-known was The Cellar, a place in the basement of a downtown building that was opened by Pat Kirkwood, whose father, W. C. Kirkwood, ran a gambling club on Jacksboro Highway. The Cellar was somewhat more louche than the Black Beret. Customers sat on cushions at low tables and waitresses wearing bikinis served mixed drinks to favored customers as well as coffee. Fights were frequent and there was a team of bouncers present to protect the waitresses. Someone described it as a Fort Worth gangster's idea of a Greenwich Village coffee house. The Cellar received national publicity when it was alleged that some of John Kennedy's Secret Service men had been cavorting there the night before Kennedy's assassination. Still, Kirkwood must have been doing something right because The Cellar outlasted all other Fort Worth coffee houses, eventually becoming a music club. It finally closed in the late 1970s.

I got into the coffee house business myself. In the fall of 1959, some friends and I rented a building near the TCU campus and opened The Coffin. We painted the walls and floor black, rounded up some tables and chairs and wine bottles with candles in them, and found an old coffin which we set up on sawhorses in the foyer. We had a folk singer, a short round boy with a crew cut who favored Marty Robbins songs and could render all four and a half minutes of "El Paso" several times each night, as well as "The Ballad of the Alamo," which was nearly as long. We also had a resident beatnik poet, a discharged airman from Carswell Air Force Base who called himself Big Mike and modeled his costume and demeanor on the New York street musician Moondog. He wore a sort of monk's robe made out of old army blankets and carried a recorder in its folds. He liked to stretch out in the coffin and then rise up playing the recorder when customers appeared in the door. We had no staff; the five of us who chipped in to pay the rent took turns each night making the coffee and waiting on tables. We had a secondhand espresso machine which broke down the first week that we were in business; after that we just boiled coffee in a big pot, served it with lemon peel in little cups, and told the customers it was espresso. Unless they had been to the Black Beret they didn't know the difference.

March 26, 2009

✤ 31 ✤

WILLOW WAY

I WAS IN San Antonio a couple of weeks ago and saw a notice in the paper about an estate sale at Willow Way, the former home of architect O'Neil Ford and his wife, Wanda, so my wife and I drove out there and spent the morning wandering around the old stone-and-brick house and its grounds, picking our way among boxes of Mexican pottery and tables full of knick-knacks. It was a bitter-sweet visit. When I lived in San Antonio in the 1960s, Willow Way was the creative vortex of the city. The Fords gave wonderful par-ties there, with colored lights stringing the garden and Jim Cullum's Happy Jazz Band playing away until dawn. Every wacky and eccentric person in San Antonio found their way there, as well as a few geniuses. The Fords had a pet monkey who lived in a hot water heater closet next to the kitchen. The closet door had a sign on it that said "Please Close the Door or the Monkey Will Get Out." It seemed that the monkey was always out at the Fords' par-ties.

Ford was a man of genuine talent. He was born in the little Grayson County farming community of Pink Hill in 1905, and he always claimed that he was the last architect in Texas to become an architect through apprenticeship, rather than by going to archi-tecture school. He was a maverick in every sense of the word. Although he became one of the most prominent architects in the United States, he was a lifetime enthusiast for indigenous architec-ture—buildings built without the services of an architect. He loved the adobe buildings along the border, the little limestone houses of Castroville, the big stone German farmhouses of the Hill Country. Although most of his work was done in an era in which new synthetic materials were the choice of most architects, he passionately believed that natural, locally available materials were superior, and his best work was done in limestone and brick. He was flamboyant in his dress and personal manner. He always wore a fresh red carnation in his lapel, and for a while, he drove around San Antonio in a huge right-hand drive 1925 Bentley.

Ford first came to San Antonio in 1939 to supervise the restoration of La Villita, the neighborhood of little stone houses along the river just south of Commerce Street, and he remained a fixture in the city until his death in 1982. When he married Wanda Graham in 1940, they moved into her mother's house at Willow Way and it quickly became the intellectual center of San Antonio. Ford's brother Lynn, a talented woodworker, built a studio in the garage and produced hand-carved doors and panels there for twenty-five years. Various members of Ford's architectural firm lived in spare bedrooms. When I was going out there in the '60s, Tom Stell, who had been a friend of Ford's since the 1920s, was a part-time resident. He was a muralist and a mosaic artist who wore frayed tweed suits and affected the type of short beard and pointed mustache that one associates with Parisian artists of the 1890s, and he was given to delivering two-hour monologues on subjects ranging from Renaissance painting to the virtues of eating cabbage. There was also a menagerie of peacocks, chickens, dogs, and birds in outdoor aviaries, in addition to the monkey.

The house had been built in the early 1930s by Wanda Ford's mother, Elizabeth Graham, in a large pecan grove between San Jose Mission and the San Antonio River, and the grounds ran all the way down to the river. Much of the building material was stone taken from the mission ruins. There were no blueprints; Graham just drew lines on the ground with a stick when she wanted to add a room and her Mexican laborers started laying up walls. My wife and I wandered through those haphazard rooms, marveling at the detritus of seventy years of intense living. (Ford died in 1982, but his widow stayed on at Willow Way until her death two years ago.)

There was a shelf of bizarre-looking ceramic wall sconces cast in a backyard kiln by Tom Stell; a table full of copper bowls and tin lanterns designed by the Ford's friend Jean Byron; piles of Patzcuaro pottery; two beautiful accordions; stacks of sheet music; hundreds of books; a carved wooden figure of a hussar on horseback; and, best of all, Ford's Wooton Patent Desk, a Victorian fantasy of drawers and pigeon holes and slots that opened out on two hinged wings to surround whoever was sitting at it with innumerable filing opportunities.

The day of the estate sale was November 2, the Day of the Dead. We had originally planned to go to San Fernando Cemetery that morning to look at the grave decorations, but we ended up having a far more poignant and personal *Día de los Muertos.*

November 17, 2005

✢ 32 ✢

JOE FRANTZ, RACONTEUR

JOE FRANTZ was a professor of history at the University of Texas in the 1950s and '60s, and was my boss at the Texas State Historical Association when I worked there in 1969 and 1970. He was also my friend until his death in 1993. He was the most entertaining man I have ever known. His friendship was rewarding simply because he was so much fun to be with. Frantz loved people and his manner showed it. Gene West of Marfa once described someone to me by saying, "When you saw him in town on Saturday he made you feel that he'd come all the way into town just to see you." Joe Frantz was like that.

Frantz was an orphan, and that may have been the key to his character. He was born in Dallas in 1917 but his parents died in the 1918 flu epidemic, and his grandmother sent him to a Fort Worth orphanage, where he was adopted by a family from Weatherford. According to Frantz's biographer, David Macomb, when Frantz's adoptive father went to the orphanage to look for a boy, the sixteen-month-old Joe toddled over to him, embraced his leg, climbed up into his lap, and held on tight. Macomb traces what he calls Frantz's "expansive capacity for friendship" to this infant need for love and security, and he may be right. It certainly worked both ways. When I worked for him at the Texas State Historical Association, hardly a day went by without someone walking into the office and saying something like, "I was just passing by on the interstate and thought I'd stop in to see Joe."

Frantz grew up in Weatherford and went to the University of Texas, where he got a BA in journalism and an MA in history before enlisting in the navy during World War II. After the war, he went back to UT for a PhD and he became a protégée of Walter Prescott Webb, who supervised his dissertation on early Texas entrepreneur Gail Borden and then hired him to teach in the UT history department. His dissertation was published in 1951 under the title *Gail Borden, Dairyman to a Nation.* It was followed in 1955 by *The American Cowboy: The Myth and the Reality*, which he coauthored with Julian Choate, an English professor, and in 1961 by *6,000 Miles of Fence: Life on the XIT Ranch of Texas*, which he wrote with Cordelia Sloan Duke, whose husband was the last manager of the XIT. These three books established Frantz's reputation as a Western historian, although he was never in Webb's category and never pretended to be. He was best at working with someone else's research, drawing insights from it, and writing it up in short, sparkling sentences.

Frantz enjoyed talking far more than he did writing, and his stories had the same quality as his sentences. He was a small, round man with a high-pitched, somewhat nasal voice and a West Texas accent, and he would start a story in a low tone accompanied by an intense look that implied that he was about to give you an extremely private piece of information. When he got to the punch line, however, his face would break into a huge grin. I had lunch with him about once a month through most of the 1970s, usually in the bar of the Driskill Hotel and frequently with several other friends. We could always tell when a story was coming by the way Frantz would hunch over the table and frown, as if he were trying to remember where he had left his car keys.

It was over one of these lunches that Frantz told us about the Princess Liechtenstein. The princess was a Weatherford girl, *née* Aleene McFarland, the daughter of a local rancher. Sometime in the late 1920s, Mr. McFarland took his family on a tour of Europe, and Aleene met and fell in love with one of the many princes of Liechtenstein. Liechtenstein is a tiny country between Switzerland and Austria, and all of the male descendants of the reigning prince bear the title of Prince, so at any given moment there are a dozen or so Princes of Liechtenstein. Aleene McFarland's prince was Prince Johannes, and they were married in London in 1931. But, according to Frantz, it turned out that they had not seriously discussed their life's ambitions before marriage. Aleene McFarland had been brought up reading the Graustark novels and *The Prisoner of Zenda,* and she thought it would be perfectly wonderful to be a princess and live in a castle. Prince Johannes, on the other hand, had been brought up on Buffalo Bill dime novels and his lifetime dream was to own a ranch in Texas and be a cowboy. The marriage did not last long, and by the time it was over, Prince Johannes had become an American citizen, changed his name to John Liechtenstein, and settled down to raise turkeys in Weatherford, and Aleene had moved into the Worth Hotel in Fort Worth, where she continued to be the Princess Liechtenstein and was a fixture in the lobby for many years.

Unlike many raconteurs, Frantz had virtually no ego. He loved to tell about the time that he shared a cab from La Guardia Airport to downtown Manhattan with Luci Johnson. The cabdriver recognized Luci and talked to her all the way to her hotel. After he let her off, he turned to Frantz to ascertain his destination and said, "You're not anybody important, are you?"

"Since then," Frantz would conclude, "I've known exactly where I stood."

Frantz's major contribution to scholarship lies not in his books but in the Lyndon B. Johnson Oral History Project, which he directed from 1968 until 1974, overseeing a staff that collected about seven hundred interviews with associates of President Johnson. No one can write about the Johnson administration without listening to these interviews. Somehow it seems appropriate that a man who loved good talk would leave a legacy that consists of people talking.

November 9, 2006

✣ 33 ✣

THE SAN ANTONIO RIVER WALK

I WAS NOT ABLE to attend the meeting in Marfa at which the Texas Tech architecture students presented proposals for rebuilding Marfa, but I enjoyed reading James Tierney's account of it in the *Big Bend Sentinel*. Had I been there, I would have risen in the interest of historical accuracy to correct a statement made by Midland architect Mark Wellen, who was quoted as saying in response to the proposal for a Marfa river walk that San Antonio's River Walk "also began with a dry riverbed." Nothing could be farther from the truth, and because the San Antonio River Walk is Texas's most important—and most enjoyable—public works project, I'd like to tell its story, even if it is not likely to be replicated in Marfa.

San Antonio's River Walk actually began with a devastating flood on the San Antonio River, which wound in a big horseshoe-shaped loop through the city's downtown business district and was wet enough for citizens to swim in, do their laundry in, and occasionally drown in. In 1921, rains upstream caused a flood that created a lake nine feet deep in downtown San Antonio and resulted in fifty deaths. The engineers immediately went to work to make sure that never happened again. Their proposals included building a cutoff channel across the neck of the downtown bend.

The original plan was for the cutoff channel only to be used during floods; in normal times, the river would flow through the downtown bend. But several developers stepped forward with the idea of permanently diverting the river into the cutoff channel and filling in the old river bed; they argued that 294,000 square feet of developable land, worth millions of dollars, could be obtained in this way. The San Antonio Conservation Society and the City Federation of Woman's Clubs came up with a counter-proposal to beautify the downtown bend with grass and trees. While the argument was going on, a young architect, Harvey Harold Hugman, came forth with a third alternative, which he called "The Shops of Aragon and Romula." Hugman's vision, perhaps inspired by the canals of Venice overlaid with a heavy dose of pseudo-Hispanic romanticism, eventually became the River Walk, but it took the New Deal and the WPA to make it happen. Hugman presented his ideas in a set of beautiful watercolors, now in the archives of the San Antonio Conservation Society, which showed people in gondolas passing under arched bridges while diners watched them from sidewalk cafes on the river's banks. But it was the depths of the Depression, and the city was broke. A group of citizens formed an Improvement District, which issued $75,000 worth of bonds, and Congressman Maury Maverick engineered a matching Works Progress Administration grant of $450,000. (Franklin Roosevelt reportedly told his Secretary of the Interior, Harold Ickes, to "give Maury the money for his damned river so he will stop bothering me.")

Work started in March of 1939 with one thousand WPA employees building bridges, limestone retaining walls, and flagstone sidewalks. Part of the charm of the River Walk lies in the fact that there were a number of Hispanic stone masons and bricklayers among the work crews, and they used their traditional skills to interpret the architect's plans. It took almost exactly two years to complete the work, which resulted in 17,000 feet of walkways, bridges, fountains, benches, flower beds, and the Arneson River Theatre, an amphitheatre with the river separating the seats from the stage. It took even longer for Hugman's vision of shops and restaurants to be fulfilled. The first restaurant on the River Walk, Casa Rio, opened in 1946, and when I moved to San Antonio twenty years later to go to work for HemisFair, the River Walk was still fairly sleepy.

It was HemisFair, the 1968 San Antonio World's Fair, that made the River Walk the vibrant place that it is today. The fairgrounds included a new convention center, and H. B. Zachary built the twenty-one-story, 480-room Palacio del Rio Hotel on the river to house convention visitors. Other hotels followed; bars and restaurants opened to accommodate their guests; and the River Walk became such a success that it was extended several times. Today the San Antonio Convention and Visitors' Bureau estimates that about six million people a year visit the River Walk. If you go there during Fiesta, you will think they are all there at once.

My friends and I spent a lot of time on the River Walk when we were working for HemisFair. One of our favorite places was a restaurant called the Poco Loco, which had an enclosed terrace that hung out over the river by the Presa Street Bridge. One night, six or eight of us were there with a somewhat tiresome visitor from New York who was trying to sell something to the Fair Corporation and had tagged along for dinner with us. We ordered a couple of plates of nachos, and the New Yorker asked what nachos were. One of our group, an architect with a whimsical sense of humor, explained that nachos were a type of shellfish that were only found in the San Antonio River. "In fact," he said, "if you get up early enough in the morning you can see the fishermen wading in the river with big butterfly nets, seining for nachos."

Our New York friend allowed that he was allergic to shellfish and passed on the nachos when they arrived, but the phrase "seining for nachos" became a byword in our crowd for a futile enterprise or a forlorn hope, as in, "If you think there will ever be a river walk in Marfa, you're just seining for nachos."

June 1, 2006

✤ 34 ✤

TEXAS-GERMAN CHRISTMASES

WHEN I LIVED IN Round Top, over in Fayette County, Christmas was an explosive event. Round Top was a German community and Germans, at least in Texas, like to hold on to old customs. When I moved there in 1970, even though my neighbors' forebears had come from Germany to Texas in the 1850s, I was the only person in town who had not grown up speaking German. Shortly after I arrived, a new Lutheran pastor suggested a minor innovation in the church's annual congregational picnic—something like serving strawberry ice cream in addition to chocolate and vanilla—and he was told in no uncertain terms, "The way we're going to do it is the way we've always done it." It sounds even more final in German. That could have been a motto for the whole community.

Until the 1950s, wedding invitations in Round Top were delivered in what my neighbors called "the old-fashioned way." This meant that the bride's father and brothers and their friends mounted up on horses whose manes and tails had been braided with red ribbons and rode from farm to farm to invite their neighbors. They carried with them a big cardboard shield on which had been written, in German script, the words "You are invited to the wedding." It was considered impersonal and impolite to send out printed invitations. By the time I moved there, this custom had fallen by the wayside, but weddings were still followed by dances which were public events, advertised by posters, at which the bride's father was expected to provide beer, barbecue and music for four to five hundred people. The dance was always opened by a grand march in which an older couple who knew the ropes led the guests around the dance floor in an intricate pattern that terminated with everyone in a circle around the bride and groom. The band would then play a waltz, and the bride and groom would have the first dance together while everyone in the circle swayed in time to the music.

There was still one family in the community, the Zwernemanns, who practiced the custom of asking friends to sit up all night in the living room with the corpse when a family member died. The Zwernemanns were a large family, and whenever a Zwernemann died, other folks were reluctant to answer their phone for a few days, for fear they were being tapped for corpse duty.

But to go back to Christmas. Most families in Round Top kept Christmas in the old-fashioned German way, which meant that Christmas started not on the day after Thanksgiving but on Christmas Eve. The holiday was foreshadowed, however, by a visit from Santa Claus on December 6, the Feast of St. Nicholas. Before World War II, Santa Claus would go from farm to farm on the night of the sixth, accompanied by his sidekick, Black Peter, whose face was blacked with cork and who took down the names of boys and girls who had been bad during the year, candidates for lumps of coal and switches. By the 1970s, a more benevolent Santa Claus, without Black Peter, paid a visit to the town square on the sixth and asked children what they wanted for Christmas. Santa Claus was always played by Milton Schlabach, a little round pink-faced fellow who was a retired farmer and made cedar porch swings in his spare time. One year word got out among the younger children just before the event that Santa Claus was not really Santa but Milton Schlabach. Milton found out about it and gave his beard and Santa suit to his wife, who was built exactly like him, and then paraded around the square in his bib overalls while Mrs. Schlabach took the children on her knee, and everyone went back to believing in Santa again.

On the afternoon of Christmas Eve the men of each family would go out in the woods and cut a Christmas tree, usually a cedar. While the children were distracted, the tree would be smuggled into the house and set up in the living room, the door of which was then closed. A male relative, usually an uncle, would climb into the room through an unlocked window and decorate the tree and arrange the presents under it while the rest of the family was at church or visiting other relatives. After supper, the door would be opened, revealing the tree and the presents in all their splendor, apparently the work of a mysterious Santa Claus who had stealthily visited the house. While the children opened the presents, the older members of the family would sip glasses of whiskey and sing some of the old Christmas songs—"Tannenbaum" or "O Du Froeliche"—and then the men would go out in the yard and fire off pistols and shotguns. This was the explosive part. You could tell exactly when each family in the community had opened their presents by noting where the gunshots were coming from.

I think of those years in Round Top whenever I see Christmas decorations going up on the weekend after Halloween. We've made Christmas longer, but I don't think we've made it any better.

December 22, 2005

BILL DODSON, CANDELILLERO

THE OTHER DAY I sat at a kitchen table in Alpine and talked with a man not much older than I am who grew up in the nineteenth century. By this I don't mean that he was born before 1900 — in fact, he was born in 1936 — but that he grew up in the same conditions that prevailed in the Big Bend in the 1880s. His name is William Dodson, and he is the father of Presidio County Sheriff Ronny Dodson. Shortly after we started talking, he showed me a photograph of his parents' first home below the Chisos Rim, on his grandfather's ranch near Dodson Spring. It consisted of a rock-walled dugout with a sotol roof and a tent pitched beside it. Even though the picture was taken in 1930, the only twentieth-century object in it is a Model T Ford in the background.

Dodson's father, Dell Dewey Dodson, died when Dodson was two, and his mother, who was twenty-three, married a sixteen-year-old *vaquero* from across the river named Sotero Morin. "He had green eyes," Dodson told me, "a *guero*." The remarriage so trauma-tized Dodson that he couldn't talk until he was ten years old, and he still speaks with a slight lilt. His stepfather had a hard time get-ting work on ranches during the Depression, and so when Dodson was seven, the family started making candelilla wax for a living. Candelilla wax, Dodson explained, is the substance that coats the tube-like leaves of the candelilla plant, and after it is refined, it has a number of industrial uses ranging from cosmetics to waterproof-ing. During World War II, he said, it was used to coat the hulls of ships.

For seven years Dodson and his three siblings lived with their parents in a tent in a series of candelilla camps in southern

Brewster County. They had a wagon and twelve burros, and every day they would go out to pull candelilla plants up. They pulled the plants up with both hands, roots and all, all day long. "We worked like dogs," Dodson told me. They tied the plants into bundles with rope and loaded them on the burros, four bundles per burro, and at the end of the day drove the burros back to the camp and stacked the bundles. After two or three weeks of pulling, they would have a stack "as high as a house," as Dodson put it, and he showed me a photograph to prove it. Then they would spend four or five days cooking the wax off the plants.

This was done in a metal vat that was buried in the ground at the camp. The one the Dodsons used was about eight feet long, four feet wide, and four feet deep, and was made in Alpine by a man named King. "It had his name stamped on it," Dodson said. It had a hole scooped out under it for a fire, which was started with wood and then fed with the remnants of the cooked plants. Dodson's mother and sisters hauled buckets of water from a spring to fill the vat, and then the plants were tossed in and stomped down. When the water started to boil, a little sulfuric acid was added to the vat, and the wax started to float up to the surface. "It looks just like oatmeal swelling up," Dodson said. It was skimmed off with a perforated dipper and tossed into a fifty-five-gallon drum, where it hardened into chunks that could be taken to the refinery in gunny sacks. The refinery was in Alpine, at the Casner Motor Company, a sort of sideline to their automobile business.

The Dodsons moved camp seven times while the children were growing up, loading their vat into their wagon, hitching two of the burros to it and driving the rest along behind. The wax business worked on a sort of sharecropping system, with the ranchers who owned the land the Dodsons were pulling the plants from providing them with the sulphuric acid and a few basic groceries like beans, rice, flour, vermicelli, and canned tomatoes and taking a share of the wax sales. I asked Dodson what they did for meat and he grinned and said, "We had deer meat year round." Once in a while, he added, a rancher would give them a goat. They bought sugar and coffee in Mexico, he said, because it was cheaper. His older sister Mildred did the cooking and washing.

Dodson told me that when he was twelve years old he had been pulling up candelilla and making wax for five years and that he could outwork any man on the river. He has taken good care of himself. Today, at seventy, he looks like a man of forty-five. In fact, when I pulled up to his house and saw him standing in the carport, I thought I was at the wrong house, expecting to see a much older man. He is tall, lean, and wiry, with a bushy head of black hair tinged with gray, a narrow face, and very blue eyes. He told me that last month he had hiked twelve miles in the Dead Horse Mountains with one of the rangers from Big Bend National Park. "I know that park like the back of my hand," he said.

Dodson's family quit making wax when he was fourteen and settled down in a house at Double Mills, and Dodson finally started on his path into the twentieth century. At sixteen, he started school at Panther Junction and learned to read and write (he had started in the first grade at Marathon when he was seven, but the teacher sent him back home because he couldn't talk) and also to have fun. "I never had fun until I went to school," he says. When he was eighteen he joined the air force, and then went on to a thirty-year career with the Texas Highway Department.

Looking back on his life, Dodson says, "There's lots of ranchers that'll tell you that they made wax, but the fact is that it was the Mexicans that did it while they watched. I'm the only Anglo that ever made wax down here, and I'll tell you, I didn't volunteer."

April 25, 2006

✤ 36 ✤

LUIS JIMÉNEZ,
ARTIST IN FIBERGLASS

FLAGS WERE FLOWN at half-mast all over New Mexico last week to honor a Texan, which was odd because Texans are not generally held in great esteem in New Mexico. But the artist Luis Jiménez, a native of El Paso, was an exceptional Texan and an exceptional man. His death on June 13 will be mourned not only by everyone who knew him but by everyone who saw and was moved by his monumental brightly-colored fiberglass sculptures, like *Lagartos* in the plaza at El Paso. Ironically, his death was caused by a piece of one of those sculptures, a thirty-two foot high rearing mustang, falling on him as it was being moved from his studio in Hondo, New Mexico.

I first met Luis Jiménez in El Paso in the early 1980s, when I wanted to borrow his fiberglass statue *Vaquero* for an exhibit on cowboys that I was doing for the Library of Congress. I called him from Santa Fe and told him that I was going to be in El Paso the following Friday and would like to meet with him to discuss the loan. He told me that he always reserved Fridays for a family lunch at a local restaurant with his father and his sister, but that I would be welcome to join them and we could go to his studio afterward and talk about the *Vaquero* loan.

I felt honored to be included in a family occasion. I knew that Jiménez's father had come to El Paso from Mexico in 1925 by wading the Rio Grande and eventually became an American citizen and a respected El Paso businessman, and I knew that he owned a neon sign factory, which was where his son had first learned welding and metalworking. Over lunch, the elder Jiménez told me with a shy smile that he considered himself an artist just like his son, and that his masterpiece was a multi-colored neon rooster on a fried chicken restaurant in Las Cruces that bent down to peck at the ground and then straightened up and threw its head back to crow. Luis later told me that when he decided to drop out of the architecture program at the University of Texas at El Paso and change his major to art, his father more or less disowned him, and they did not speak to each other for several years. However, when he had his first gallery exhibit in New York in 1967, he received a package from his father. Inside was a gold watch engraved with the words, "To my son the artist." When we left the restaurant that day and got into Luis's car to go his studio, Luis lit a cigarette and said, "You know, I'm forty-two years old and a successful artist and I still can't bring myself to light up a cigarette in front of my father." His sculpture, *Border Crossing*, which depicts a man wading the river with his wife and child on his back, is a tribute to his father.

Luis was happy to loan *Vaquero* to my exhibit. The sixteen-and-a-half-foot statue of a Mexican American cowboy waving a pistol from the back of a blue bucking bronco looked fabulous in the cold and colorless marble hall of the Library of Congress's James Madison Building, a building so infelicitous that it is known as the box that the Sam Rayburn Building—universally acknowledged as the ugliest building in Washington—came in. I wanted something that would draw visitors into the building and let them know that there was an exhibit about cowboys back in its recesses, and *Vaquero* filled the bill perfectly.

Luis was a quiet and gentle person, but his sculpture always seemed to attract controversy. For one thing, he worked in a non-traditional material, fiberglass sprayed with acrylic aircraft paint and covered with several coats of clear polyurethane varnish, which he felt perfectly suited his subject matter, images drawn largely from Mexican American popular culture. He thought the surfaces of his sculpture replicated the surfaces of the lowrider automobiles that had fascinated him as a young man. For another, some people found his images threatening, or, in the polite language of city councils, "inappropriate." His *Vaquero* was rejected by two sites because some people objected to the cowboy's pistol. "No one would dream of taking away Robert E. Lee's gun or George Washington's sword," he was quoted as saying, "but somehow a Mexican with a gun is seen as a big threat."

About the time that I met Luis, he was commissioned to create a sculpture for a park in Albuquerque's Old Town, the site of the original eighteenth-century plaza of Albuquerque, now surrounded by souvenir shops and fast-food restaurants catering to tourists. He produced a massive fiberglass work called *Southwest Pietà*, depicting an Aztec warrior holding the scantily-clad corpse of an Aztec lady in his arms with the snowy peak of a volcano rising behind them. The statue referred to the Aztec legend of the lovers Popocatepetl and Ixtaccihuatl, who were turned into volcanoes by the gods, as depicted on Mexican calendars. But when it was unveiled, all hell broke loose. The city council thought it would offend tourists; Hispanics who traced their descent from old Spanish families thought it was "too Mexican"; a rumor started that it depicted the rape of an Indian by a Spaniard. Eventually it was moved to a park in a working class neighborhood called Martineztown, which suited Luis just fine. He always said that he wanted his art to be seen by people who couldn't afford to buy it. And it can be, because it is in public places from Houston to Boston to Fargo, North Dakota, to the Smithsonian Institution, a pretty good record for the son of an illegal immigrant.

June 22, 2006

✦ 37 ✦

DESERT RAIN

SEVERAL WEEKS AGO, a couple of hours before sunset, my wife and I were driving from Fort Davis to Marfa. The sky in the west had been full of threatening black clouds all afternoon, and when we came over the Divide we looked out over the Marfa Flats and saw a great sleeve of rain off to our right, what in Mexico is called a *manga de agua*. It was a semi-transparent white, almost like a cylinder of fog reaching up to the sky, and through it we could see a streak of white smoke hugging the ground, probably a grass fire started by a lightning strike. As we drove around the edge of it, we could smell the wetness in the air, a sharp, pungent, almost chemical smell. There were two more sleeves in the east, over toward Cathedral Mountain, one of them full of lightning bolts that crackled down to the ground every few seconds. Coming back to Fort Davis, just at sunset, we were driving straight toward a storm over the Davis Mountains. We could see the eastern edge of it, a vertical line in the sky, black on one side, light gray on the other, lightning to the left, calm to the right. We were literally *al filo de la agua*, on the edge of the storm, as Augustin Yáñez called his great novel about the Mexican Revolution. Later that night we sat on our roof deck and watched lightning flash over Sleeping Lion Mountain. That storm was off to the north, somewhere between Fort Davis and Balmorhea.

All of this got me to thinking about how different rain in the desert is from rain in the city. Rain in the desert is elemental and fundamental, and we are always glad to see it. Last year, when we seemed to be getting an abnormal amount of rain, I asked a rancher friend in Marfa if he thought we could get too much rain. "You will never hear me say that! Never!" he replied. He was quite emphatic about it. In the city, no one is grateful for rain. It just means overflowing gutters, wet feet, inconvenience for everyone. For some reason, you never seem to see lightning in the city. The buildings block it out.

I happen to think that lightning is the most beautiful of all natural phenomena, but I can watch it through a window. The nineteenth-century cowboys who took herds up the trail to Kansas hated it. Its immediacy was terrifying to a man out on the prairie on horseback, and it caused stampedes that could take days to untangle. Some cowboys became connoisseurs of lightning. G. W. Mills of Lockhart described a storm he was in near Ogallala, Nebraska, in 1879 in his contribution to J. Marvin Hunter's *The Trail Drivers of Texas*: "It first commenced with flash lightning, then came forked lightning, then chain lightning, followed by the peculiar blue lightning. After that show it rapidly developed into ball lightning, which rolled along the ground. After that spark lightning, then, most wonderful of all, it settled down on us like a fog. The air smelled of burning sulphur; you could see it on the horns of the cattle, the ears of our horses, and the brims of our hats. It grew so warm we thought we might burn up with it."

My wife and I once saw a type of lightning that Mills missed in his description. We were driving west out of Nashville, Tennessee, at about four-thirty in the morning on one of our annual trips to Fort Worth to visit my parents. It was raining cats and dogs, a spring storm. Suddenly there was a tremendous clap of thunder and a coil of lightning that looked exactly like a giant roll of barbed wire unfurled across the sky in front of us. I have never seen anything else like it in my life. It left a green after-impression in front of my eyes that lasted at least sixty seconds.

It was not just nineteenth-century cowboys who had encounters with lightning. Gene West of Marfa once told me about rounding up a herd in a big pasture in the Panhandle in the 1960s. He and his hands were working in a rainstorm, trying to gather about three hundred steers to ship to a buyer. Through the rain, he saw a line of about twenty animals standing stock still, head to tail. He thought that was peculiar, and when he rode closer, he saw that they were all leaning against a fence and they were all dead. They had evidently drifted against the fence in the storm and were all touching it when lightning struck it. "Each one weighed about nine hundred pounds," West said. "That lightning really took the cream off the sale."

Sometimes it can rain too much, even in West Texas. I was in Fort Worth in the summer of 1949, visiting my grandmother, when it rained for two weeks without stopping. The Trinity River overflowed its banks and there was water up to the second story of the Montgomery Ward building on West 7th Street. Of course it didn't rain again in Fort Worth, or anywhere in West Texas, for seven more years. My father made a highway inspection trip to West Texas in January of 1956 and stayed for several nights in a motel in Monahans. When he got back home, I asked him what Monahans was like. "Well, I'll tell you," he said. "When Noah got rain for forty days and forty nights, Monahans got half an inch."

My friend Judy Burgess of Terlingua grew up in Anson, Texas, during those dry years. When the drought finally broke, she saw the first rain she had ever seen in her young life. The only rain she knew about was Noah's, as described in the family Bible, and she was extremely worried because she knew her family did not have a boat. Come to think of it, that may be why she ended up moving to Terlingua.

July 27, 2006

✛ 38 ✛

FORTY-TWO

THE SUMMER AFTER I graduated from high school, I got a job as a rodman on a Texas Highway Department survey party and I started learning about life. I did not exactly have a sheltered childhood, but it was definitely a middle-class one, and I had never met anyone like the men I worked with on that survey party before. I earned $110 a month, which in 1957 was pretty good for a seventeen-year-old kid who was living at home and had no responsibilities, but some of the men on the party were supporting families on that amount. One of them had a sick wife and baby at home, and our party chief, a goodhearted man called G. W., who was a Missionary Baptist preacher in his spare time, broke all of the highway department's rules and let the man bring a .22 rifle along on the job and shoot rabbits at lunch time in order to put meat on his dinner table.

Another fellow worker, a tall, rangy old boy named Ferris Hendricks, supplemented his income by playing guitar in a hillbilly band that played in bars and occasionally appeared in Cowtown Hoedown at the Majestic Theatre. He belonged to some Pentecostal church that did not hold with playing music in honkytonks, and he worried a good deal about that, but he couldn't keep away from them. Hendricks had long sideburns, which he claimed he had grown before Elvis Presley popularized them. He also claimed that he had written "Crazy Arms" and that Ray Price had stolen it from him, so every time we stopped in a café we had to play "Crazy Arms" on the juke box for him, usually several times.

We didn't stop in cafés often, because we usually ate our lunches on the job. We spent most of the summer running a survey line for a new farm-to-market road that crossed the Trinity River west of Forth Worth, and we could usually find a big shady tree in the river bottom to eat lunch under. A morning ritual was stopping at a 7-Eleven store on the way to the job to pick out our lunchtime soft drinks. I favored Dr Pepper, but my colleagues all drank RC Cola. RC had just come out with a new bottle shape that summer, a faceted bottle with about a dozen sides, and there was a continuing discussion on the survey party about whether RC tasted better in the old round bottles or the new faceted ones. Each member of the party would have to fish around in the ice-cold water of the soft drink cooler at the 7-Eleven until they found the bottle that suited them, so it took us longer to get on the road than most parties. We also bought ripe plums at the 7-Eleven, wrapped them in tinfoil, and dropped them into the water cooler that we carried in the back of the station wagon. I have never tasted anything since then that was as good as an ice-cold plum on a hot summer day.

I learned a great deal from the men I worked with that summer, some of which is best not retold in a family newspaper. I learned how to drive a stick-shift automobile, because the nearest pay telephone to our job was in a liquor store on Benbrook Highway, and G. W. knew enough about human nature not to send an overheated man who was old enough to buy alcohol into a place that sold cold beer. So if a call had to be made back to the resident engineer's office, I was the designated telephoner. I had learned to drive in our family's 1955 De Soto, which had an automatic transmission, and the first time I got in the station wagon I was embarrassed to admit I didn't know how to shift the gears, and so it bucked and stalled until G. W. showed me how to use the clutch and gearshift.

I also learned how to play a domino game called Forty-Two, and that is the real subject of this reminiscence. Every day at lunch we would take a square of plywood out of the station wagon, set it on top of a wooden crate that was also kept in there, and hunker down on our heels around it for thirty minutes of Forty-Two. Forty-Two was known as the national game of the Texas Highway Department, and there was something comforting in knowing that as we were shuffling the dominoes, survey parties and maintenance crews all over the state were doing exactly the same thing, much in the same way that all schoolchildren in France are learning the same lesson at the same time each day.

Forty-Two, for you new Texans, is a four-handed domino game that involves bidding, trumps, and taking tricks, a sort of simplified form of bridge. It seems to have originated in Texas in the 1880s, and while there are a variety of creation myths concerning it, they all seem to agree that its beginnings have to do with the sinfulness of playing cards—the devil's picture book, as the hardshell Baptists called them—or the illegality of playing card games in public places. My mother told me that Forty-Two was invented because it was against the law to play cards on trains in Texas, and so certain wily Texans figured out a way to gamble on dominoes. Paul Proft, a San Antonio Forty-Two enthusiast who has a website about the game at http://texas42.net (one of several such sites), told me about a 1985 story in the *Fort Worth Star-Telegram* that pinpoints its origin in Garner, Texas, in 1887, when two boys were caught playing cards in the barn by their Baptist parents and, smarting from their punishment, invented Forty-Two. On the other hand, Halletsville, Texas, about 250 miles southeast of Garner, claims to be the cradle of Forty-Two. It doesn't really matter where it was born; it grew to be a robust adult and it's a great way to pass a lunch hour or a cold winter evening.

September 28, 2006

✤ 39 ✤

KING WILLIAM STREET

THERE IS A tree-shaded street just south of San Antonio's business district that is only five blocks long, but there is more history packed into those five blocks than most Texas towns can boast of. It has a flour mill at one end of it and a little park with a bandstand at the other, and in the 1870s it was named King William Street after King William of Prussia, Kaiser Wilhelm's grandfather. A hundred years before that, the land it runs across was part of the lower farm of the Mission San Antonio de Valero, better known as the Alamo. The mission's fields were watered by the San Antonio River, which flows right behind some of the big houses at the lower end of the street. The river is why Carl Hilmar Guenther built his Pioneer Flour Mill there and it is why the street became such a fashionable neighborhood in the 1880s and '90s.

When I lived on King William Street in the 1960s, it was far from fashionable. Most of the big old houses had been divided into apartments, and some had been given over to institutional uses. I had an apartment that occupied about a third of the ground floor of a house that had been built in 1890; just down the street was an old mansion that had been turned into a halfway house for mental patients, where an intense-looking young man spent his afternoons throwing a hatchet at a target nailed to a tree in the side yard. Around the corner was another rambling old house that was a sort of upscale flop house for winos. In the mornings they sat on the front porch and sipped their wine discreetly from coffee cups. In the evenings they congregated in the back yard and drank openly from bottles. But mixed in with the derelicts and mental patients was a population of creative young people who had come to San Antonio to work for HemisFair, the 1968 San Antonio World's Fair. O'Neil Ford's architectural office was at the end of the street, and some of the apartments were occupied by young architects who worked for him. Others were the homes of designers, graphic artists, special event producers, and other members of the floating population that followed world's fairs. We did a lot of visiting back and forth and had the kind of good times that unattached young people have in a big city.

Last week I went to the Brazos Forum in Waco and heard a presentation on the history of King William Street given by an old friend from those days, Maria Watson Pfeiffer. Pfeiffer's great-grandfather, Carl Groos, built his house on King William Street in 1881. Her grandmother and her mother grew up in the Groos house, and after her mother married, she and Pfeiffer's father bought a cousin's house two blocks away that had been built in 1860. Pfeiffer grew up in that house, and she and her husband still live there. As she said in her presentation, she has not moved very far or very fast in four generations. Pfeiffer's family is typical of the German merchants who built homes along King William Street in the late nineteenth century; their children often lived near them, and sometimes even their grandchildren.

In her presentation, Pfeiffer explained that while the original developers of the neighborhood were the Nova Scotia-born Devine brothers, it was the Germans who gave the neighborhood its distinctive stamp. Carl Hilmar Guenther built his mill at the end of the street in 1859, and his sons and sons-in-law built their homes in the block nearest the mill. Successful lumber dealer Edward Steves built his stone mansion on the next block in 1877, and the Joskes, Kalteyers, and Oppenheimers soon followed. There was an indoor natatorium in the back yard of the Steves home, as they did not think their children should swim with ordinary children in the river. Pfeiffer said that by her mother's time, the neighborhood children were all welcome to swim in the natatorium, but at 2:00 p.m. a bell would be rung, which was the signal for them to make themselves scarce as Mrs. Steves was about to appear for her afternoon dip. Pfeiffer's talk was illustrated with wonderful old photographs, one of which showed a group of King William Street ladies gathered for a coffee klatsch on the porch of the Groos house about 1900, while another showed their daughters and granddaughters gathered around a Christmas tree in another King William Street house sixty years later.

In September of 1918 the San Antonio City Council, in a fit of patriotic fervor, voted to change the name of King William Street to Pershing Street, but the name only stuck for a couple of years. In 1921, thirty-two of the forty-one residents of the street appeared before the City Council and petitioned that the name be changed back. "We are not opposed to General Pershing," one of them said, "but we love the name of King William Street and want it back."

Not all of the early residents were German. One of the finest houses in the neighborhood was built by a retired British diplomat, George Chabot. Chabot's grandson, Frederick Chabot, after an unsuccessful career in the US Diplomatic Corps in South America, became San Antonio's premier antiquarian. He founded the city's first local historical group, the Yanaguana Society, and in the 1930s he published several important books on San Antonio's past. He financed his publications by the subscription method, and roamed up and down King William Street knocking on doors in search of subscribers. He was evidently not a frequent bather, and when I lived on the street he was still remembered by some residents as Smelly Fred.

In the 1970s King William Street was rediscovered, and today most of its houses have been restored by affluent San Antonians. But the neighborhood still retains more than a whiff of its raffish character. As Gary Cartwright said in a *Texas Monthly* article about King William Street several years ago, the street has not succumbed to gentrification but "is practically reeling with eccentrification—about a century's worth."

October 12, 2006

✤ 40 ✤

TIGIE LANCASTER'S MULES

LAST YEAR AT THE St. Paul's Episcopal Church ice cream social in Marfa, a woman with a ruddy compelexion, short gray hair, and very blue eyes drove up to the church in a rubber-tired buckboard pulled by a mule. She asked a small boy standing at the curb to go in and get her a dish of ice cream, and then sat in the buckboard and ate it. Her name is Tigie Lancaster, and she has lived in Marfa since 1998. The mule's name was Hollywood Doc. Well, actually, it was just Doc, but Lancaster says that he had been in so many movies that she called him Hollywood Doc. Doc, who died last spring, was a big mule, sixteen-and-a-half hands high. His mother was a Kentucky thoroughbred mare and his father was a Mammoth jack. "He was the mule of my dreams," Lancaster told me the other day. "He was everything you would want in a mule." When I asked her exactly what she meant by that, she said, "Not many mules would let you put a tutu on him." Then I remembered that Doc was the mule that Lancaster entered in the Beautiful Burro and Mule Contest in Fort Davis last year. He not only wore a tutu, but also had simulated ballet slippers on his hooves. Doc had other good qualities, too, according to Lancaster: "He had a superior attitude around horses—you could see that he didn't approve of their kicking and running around. He was real smooth—he didn't have any rough, bouncy qualities. He was unflappable. He was a special mule."

Although Lancaster is basically a horse person, she has had a lot of experience with mules. When she was a child in Dallas, she was fascinated by the mules that pulled the garbage wagon through her neighborhood, and she persuaded the garbage man to let her climb up beside him when he came by and ride to the end of the block. Her grandmother was horrified, but her mother said, "There's no point in telling her not to do it. She'll just do it anyway," which seems to have been a pattern in Lancaster's life. A few years later, when she was at a girls' boarding school in Colorado Springs, she was introduced to an army mule named Hambone who could jump with thoroughbreds. She sometimes went foxhunting with the El Paso County Hounds, and one of the army officers at Camp Carson used to bring Hambone along on fox hunts. He could sail over fences with the best of them. Lancaster got to ride Hambone once, and she told me that it was like riding in a Rolls-Royce. Hambone became her standard of "a real doing mule."

Lancaster's first mule, however, was not up to Hambone's standards. "He was a Shetland mule, a handsome strawberry roan with white stockings," she said, "but he had a cheating heart and was not generous. He had been trained to pull but you had to retrain him every day, and if he got a chance to let you have it, he would. He was the opposite of Doc in every way." Most mules, Lancaster was quick to add, are not like that, although they are independent-minded. "Mules are smarter than horses," she said. "Horses aren't Einsteins and they can be bullied into doing things they shouldn't do, but mules don't like bullies and they won't go anywhere that isn't safe."

Mules get their good qualities from donkeys, Lancaster told me, and she is also fond of donkeys—in fact, she has four of them in her pasture right now, named Black Jack, Apple Jack, Bottom, and Pearl Lite. "The only animal I ever rustled was a donkey," she told me. This was in the late 1950s, she explained, and she had come out to the Big Bend for a short vacation. She drove her pickup to the store at Lajitas and asked the man there if she could drive on down to the river, and he told her that she had better leave her truck at the store and walk to the river, as someone might steal her hubcaps if she parked it on the river bank. She took his advice and walked through the brush to the river, where she found a donkey tethered to a tree. The donkey was saddled and bridled, and there were two big gunny sacks on the ground beside his feet. She looked in the gunny sacks and discovered they were full of hubcaps. Impulsively, she untied the donkey, got on him, and rode him along the river for a while. When she finally got back to her truck, she said, "I hated to part with him. I reasoned that anyone who was stealing hubcaps wouldn't prosecute me for stealing a donkey, so I put the tailgate down and he jumped right into my truck. I stopped in Fort Stockton and bought some stake sides and drove back to Dallas with him. I never felt guilty about taking that burro. There were plenty of them around and the guy who owned it probably would have taken my hubcaps."

Mules and donkeys are really a sideline to Lancaster, who has spent most of her life training horses and teaching riding. I asked her how she got into the horse business, and she told me that during her sophomore year at Bennington College she got interested in the writings of Eugene V. Debs, five-time Socialist candidate for president and founder of the first railroad workers union. "I came home that summer and started telling my grandfather about my admiration for Eugene V. Debs," she said. "Well, my grandfather was president of the Texas and Pacific Railroad, and he said that if that was what I was learning at Bennington he was going to take me out of there, and I could either go to Sweet Briar or the University of Texas. I said I wasn't going to either one. I had a friend in Dallas who had polo horses, so I leased a stable from him and started boarding polo ponies and training jumpers, and I've been doing that ever since." And she's been speaking her mind ever since, too.

November 2, 2006

THE SEVEN TIMMERMANN SISTERS

THE COMING of Christmas always makes me think of the seven Timmermann sisters of Geronimo, Texas, except that I think of them with initial capital letters: the Seven Timmermann Sisters, like the Three Fates or the Nine Muses. The sisters— Willie May, Estella, Mellita, Wanda, Meta, Hulda, and Thekla— became famous in the 1950s for the Christmas decorations they created in the farmhouse they all lived in at Geronimo, which is a small community between Seguin and New Braunfels. Unlike the garish urban Christmas decorations of the fifties, these did not involve brightly-lit yard displays, plastic Santa Clauses climbing into chimneys, or reindeer on the roof. Instead, the Timmermann sisters spent a week each December setting up an enormous Christmas tree in their living room and surrounding its base with an artificial landscape that reached out to cover most of the living room floor. When it was finished, they would open their house to visitors, and each year several thousand people would come by to view the scene and share coffee and German Christmas cookies with the sisters. *LIFE* magazine discovered them in the mid-1950s and carried a picture story about them, and for the next thirty years no Christmas was complete without a feature story in some magazine or newspaper about the seven Timmermann sisters. They became as much a part of the landscape of Central Texas as Hallie Stillwell was of the Big Bend.

The Timmermann sisters were born between 1895 and 1916. None ever married, and none ever left the farm they were born on, a farm their grandfather, Heinrich Timmermann, established shortly after he came to Texas from Germany in the 1840s. For

many years they operated a florist shop on the farm, serving customers in New Braunfels and Seguin. Articles about them always
included a photograph of their bedroom, a large T-shaped room
with seven beds in it, and a photograph of them in the matching
outfits they wore to Seguin High School football games and on
other occasions. That photograph usually showed them posed in
ascending order of age on a staircase. Some articles mentioned the
cookbook they published, *Seven Silver Spoons*, which was narrat-
ed by a dishpan named Dian.

Their tree was usually a cedar, cut on private land somewhere
in the area, and the cutting was a ceremony in itself. In a 1973 article in the *San Antonio Express*, George Carmack described that
year's tree-cutting expedition. The seven sisters went out to a farm
near McDade, where a neighbor had picked out a tree for them,
in a convoy that consisted of their station wagon, two pickup
trucks, a trailer, and several chainsaw-wielding neighbors. Before
the tree was cut, the group built a fire and had a picnic around it
that consisted of sausages, sauerkraut, and camp potatoes. The tree
was brought back to the Timmermann house and decorated with
ornaments (some of which had been in the family for a hundred
years), candles, and freshly baked cookies.

After the tree was decorated, the sisters laid out the landscape
around it. This consisted of honeycombed limestone rocks covered with Spanish moss which cradled miniature buildings and a
hundred or so carved wooden figures. There was an elaborate
nativity scene, and a flowing waterfall with real water representing
the Guadalupe River, and a model of the orphanage established at
New Braunfels in the late 1840s by the sisters' great-grandfather on
their mother's side, Pastor Louis Ervandberg. Wooden figures
around the orphanage represented the pastor, his wife, and the
twenty orphans who lived there. The figures, which were carved
for the sisters by a family in Germany, had movable arms and legs
and were dressed in clothes sewn by the sisters.

Their great-grandfather's orphanage played a large role in the sisters' family history, their idea of themselves, and their Christmas celebrations. They would tell its story to every reporter who interviewed them. In 1844, Ervandberg was retained by the founder of New Braunfels, Prince Carl of Solms-Braunfels, to minister to the shiploads of German immigrants who were landing at Indianola on the Texas coast and coming to New Braunfels in wagon trains. So many people died of dysentery and cholera on that trip that Ervandberg and his wife established the West Texas Orphan Asylum on the banks of the Guadalupe, a few miles from New Braunfels, to care for the children left behind. Ervandberg was a respected citizen of New Braunfels, and the orphanage flourished for several years. In the early 1850s, twenty boys and girls lived there in two dormitories. Part of the Timmermann sisters' Christmastime ceremonies involved one of the sisters reading aloud to groups of visitors an account of a visit to the orphanage at Christmas of 1849 by Hermann Seele, a New Braunfels schoolteacher. Seele described the Christmas tree at the orphanage, surrounded by honeycombed limestone rocks representing the mountains of the Holy Land with a nativity scene surmounting them, and how the boys and girls made presents for each other and exchanged them on Christmas Eve. It was a touching story, and it was clearly important to the sisters.

Only two of the Timmermann sisters are still alive, and they are both in their nineties. Last year was the last Christmas that they decorated their tree and held an open house. I have to say that I never attended their Christmas celebration, nor did I ever meet them. In fact, I always thought there was something a little weird about them and their matching outfits and their seven beds in one room and their talking dishpan, a little too much like Snow White and the Seven Dwarfs. But while I was working on this essay, I learned something that gave me a deeper understanding of them. I read the article on Pastor Ervandberg in *The New Handbook of*

Texas, and I discovered that in 1855, at the age of forty-six, he sent his wife and three daughters to St. Louis and ran off to Mexico with one of the orphans, a seventeen-year-old girl with whom he subsequently had two children. The Timmermann sisters' grandmother was one of those daughters that went to St. Louis. That might explain why the sisters never married, and maybe even why they devoted their Christmases to giving pleasure to others. Sometimes things even out that way.

December 20, 2006

✤ 42 ✤

CZECHS AND POLKAS

A FEW WEEKS AGO, at a dinner party in Fort Davis, I met Stephen Zetsche from Wharton, Texas. Zetsche's father was the Disciples of Christ minister in Marfa in the 1950s, and Zetsche was revisiting the sites of his youth with his lady friend, Ricki Boyd. Since I have a lot of cousins in Wharton County, we got to talking about some of the things that have happened there, and suddenly Zetsche was telling me about the El Campo Polka War.

It seems that Zetsche is the director of broadcasting and part owner of radio station KULP in El Campo. El Campo is about fifteen miles from Wharton and has a large Czech population, folks whose ancestors came from Moravia to Texas in the early twentieth century to grow cotton. There are so many Czechs around El Campo that the high school band plays "The Julida Polka" when El Campo secures the winning point at football games. For years KULP had played an hour of Czech polka music every weekday morning between 8:00 and 9:00 a.m. On Saturdays, the polkas started at 6:00 a.m. and ran until noon, six solid hours. Three years ago, Zetsche's two partners who lived in Austin decided that the station was playing an excessive amount of polka music and decided to drop the weekday morning program. Zetsche disagreed, but since he was outvoted two to one, he complied, and one Friday went on the air to announce that starting the following Monday the polkas would be replaced by a country-western program.

As Zetsche tells it, nothing happened for three weeks. "Then," he says, "I went to the station on Monday morning and found seventy-five geriatric Czechs on the sidewalk, some of them on walkers and some with canes. They had signs that said things like 'We Want Our Polkas Back,' 'We Love Polka,' and 'Czech It Out.' There was a van full of people from an assisted living home parked at the curb, and in front of it was an old guy playing polkas on the accordion. It had just taken three weeks for them to get organized." They were back on Tuesday, and again on Wednesday. In the meantime, Zetsche fielded angry telephone calls all day and endured a visit from a feisty woman who stalked into his office, lectured him for fifteen minutes, said, "You haven't listened to a thing I've said," and stalked out.

Finally, on Thursday, Zetsche came to work to find a single picket, a middle-aged, mild-mannered man who greeted Zetsche pleasantly, introduced himself as Richard, and said, "I'm here for my father." He explained that his father was in his eighties and bedridden and lived for 8:00 a.m. each day, when he could turn on the radio and listen to polka music. Since the polkas had gone off the air he had been desolate. Zetsche said, "I felt like we were the terrorists who pushed the man in the wheel chair off the deck of that cruise ship." He invited Richard into his office, put in a call to his Austin partners, and told them that the new format wasn't working and the polka music was going back on the air on Monday. They acquiesced, and Zetsche then put Richard on the air to announce that the polka hour would return the next Monday. The next day a group of elderly Czech ladies showed up at the station with a big sign that read "We Love KULP" and plates of the fruit-filled Czech pastries called kolaches. Today, KULP plays eleven hours of polka music a week. "And that's the way it's going to be," Zetsche told me. "I'm never going through that again."

Polka music is alive and well on radio stations all through Central Texas, which is where most of the state's Czech population is concentrated. Most of it is homemade, meaning that it is recorded by local bands like the Dujka Brothers from East Bernard or the Vrazel Polka Band from Yarrellton or Leroy Rybak's Swinging Orchestra from Hallettsville. The programs are put together by disc jockeys who sometimes work out of the local stations and sometimes out of their own homes. When I lived in Fayette County in the 1970s, the local polka king of the airwaves was Lee Roy Matocha of Fayetteville, who had a four-hour program that he put together weekly in a sound studio in his garage and that was played on fifty radio stations in Texas. Matocha had a disconcerting habit of singing along in Czech over the records he was playing, so listeners were never sure what was on the record and what was Lee Roy. His commercials were disarmingly informal, something along the line of, "Stop in at the White Auto Store in La Grange. They'll treat you right and they speak Czech, too."

Matocha had his own band, the Lee Roy Matocha Orchestra, which played at feasts, weddings, and dance halls all over Central Texas for thirty-five years until his retirement in 1998. They traveled in an old Greyhound bus that Matocha called the Golden Eagle and that had the words "You Are Now Following the Fayetteville Flash" painted across the rear end, which was slightly ironic since Matocha was a slow, deliberate man. When Matocha died suddenly at the age of seventy in 2003, he had been playing polka music professionally for fifty-six years — he started at the age of fourteen in Zbranek's Accordion Band from Plum, Texas.

My friend George Koudelka from Flatonia started when he was even younger. Koudelka, who knows more about Texas polka recordings than anyone else in the world, was playing the drums with a Flatonia band called The Shuck Brothers when he was ten. He has devoted his whole life to polka music and has played in more than a dozen bands. In a region where silver wedding anniversaries are occasions for huge parties with beer, barbecue, and music, Koudelka, a lifelong bachelor, decided in 1980 to throw a party to celebrate the twenty-fifth anniversary of his first public appearance in a band — his wedding to music, as he put it.

He hired the Round Top Rifle Hall and provided the beer and barbecue, and his friends provided the music. A thousand people showed up to honor Koudelka. If Stephen Zetsche's business partners had been there, they would never have tried to cut the Czechs of El Campo off from their polka programs.

July 12, 2007

FAYETTE COUNTY FOURTH OF JULY

YESTERDAY was the two hundred and thirty-first Fourth of July to be celebrated in the United States since bells rang out in Philadelphia to celebrate the passage of the Declaration of Independence by the Continental Congress in 1776. Actually, those first bells rang out on July 8, because although Congress passed the Declaration on the evening of the fourth, it was not publicly proclaimed until the eighth when, as John Adams wrote to a friend, bells pealed all day and all night and soldiers fired salutes on the Philadelphia common "notwithstanding the scarcity of powder." But ever since then we have celebrated Independence Day on the fourth.

In the 1970s I lived in a tiny German community called Round Top (population: 70) over in Fayette County, about halfway between Austin and Houston. The folks who lived there were notoriously sociable; in fact, a history of Fayette County published in 1910 said that "the town of Round Top is noted for the splendor of its feasts." The biggest feast of all was the Fourth of July. It was even bigger than *Schuetzenfest*, the annual meeting of the Round Top Rifle Club, at which members shot at an iron target all morning, drank beer all afternoon, and danced all night. There was an old joke in Round Top about a local boy who was being prepared for confirmation in the Lutheran Church. One of the questions in the Lutheran catechism is "What are the three great feasts of the Christian year?" to which the answer is "Christmas, Easter, and Pentecost." When this young man was asked the question he unhesitatingly responded (in German), "*Weinachtfest, Schuetzen-*

fest, und Viertenjuli" (Christmas, Shooting Feast, and the Fourth of July).

The Fourth of July has been celebrated continuously in Round Top since the town was founded in the early 1850s, and a body of folklore has grown up around the celebration, stories that are repeated every year on the Fourth. In the 1870s, part of the celebration involved firing off a cannon that had been left on the town square by Union troops who were stationed there during Reconstruction. On one memorable Fourth, a local smart aleck insisted on stuffing twice as much powder as usual down the cannon's barrel and then climbing astride it as the touch hole was lit. The barrel exploded and killed him. This was always related as a cautionary tale to small boys who were lighting firecrackers, and the remnant of the cannon, which had been buried with its stub end protruding from the grass, was pointed out as evidence of careless behavior.

Then there was the story about Nana Schulz, who died a few years before I moved to Round Top. Nana was what people in Round Top called "afflicted," meaning that he was somewhat simple. But he had been born on the Fourth of July, and he considered the Fourth his personal birthday party. For seventy years he went through the crowd watching the parade holding out his palm and saying, *"Gib mir nickel fur Geburtstag"* — "Give me a nickel for my birthday." When he died, his relatives found hundreds of dollars in nickels in a box under his bed.

The crowds on the square were large on the Fourth because the celebration served as a homecoming for everyone in Texas who had any connections with Round Top, and there were usually several thousand people in town that day. When I lived there, the ceremonies were started at 10:00 a.m. on the town square by Mayor Don Nagel, who always welcomed everyone with a short speech about "the glorious traditions of the ancient city of Round Top" and invited all present to the barbecue at the Rifle Hall after the parade. This was followed by an invocation by the Lutheran pastor, who in turn was followed by the retired school principal, John Banik, who delivered a half-hour long oration entitled "Heroes in Unmarked Graves." Banik had been giving this speech, which dealt with residents of Fayette County who had fought in the Texas Revolution, since about 1940 and most of the audience could recite it from memory. He always worried that the invocation would cut into his speaking time and invariably, just as the mayor was winding up his welcome, Banik would turn to the Lutheran pastor and say, "Listen, couldn't we have the invocation after the oration?" and the pastor would patiently explain why it couldn't be done that way.

The high point of the morning was the parade, which consisted of half a dozen floats representing organizations like the Sons of Hermann and the Do Your Duty Club, followed by everyone else in town on horseback. The Sons of Hermann float was always the same—a dozen or so Hermann Sons sitting around a table on a flatbed trailer drinking beer, getting a head start on the rest of the town. One year I rode in the parade in a full-sized replica of an 1850s Abbot & Downing Concord stagecoach, accompanied by Houston philanthropist Ima Hogg, who had a weekend home in Round Top and who had restored a historic farmstead near the town. The coach was pulled by three mules and an old mare belonging to a local farmer named Fritz Schoenst, who liked to fool with mules, but the next week the *Houston Post's* society page reported that Miss Hogg had ridden in a coach pulled by four white stallions. The society reporter was clearly not a careful observer of horseflesh.

The year that Governor Dolph Briscoe closed down Fayette County's most venerable enterprise, a bawdy house near La Grange called the Chicken Ranch, *Texas Observer* coeditors Molly Ivins and Kaye Northcott proposed putting a float in the parade that would feature them in nightgowns, reclining on a brass bedstead with flapping chickens tethered to it. They planned to toss copies of a 45 RPM record by ZZ Top entitled "La Grange" to the crowd, but the Fayette County sheriff, a nice old gentleman who had been terribly embarrassed by the whole Chicken Ranch episode, let it be known that he would prefer that they not do that, and Ivins and Northcott graciously withdrew the idea. I've always wished they'd gone ahead with it; they would have joined Nana Schulz and the careless cannoneer in Round Top Fourth of July mythology.

July 5, 2007

✣ 44 ✣

BILLY D. PEISER, EL INDIO

BILLY D. PEISER OF MARFA is the master of a profession that most people think disappeared with Daniel Boone. He is a tracker, and during his twenty-five years with the Border Patrol here, he was so good that he was known all over northern Mexico as *El Indio*. When the Border Patrol caught up with a party of illegal immigrants out in the brush, one of the immigrants would always ask, "Is *El Indio* with you?"

Peiser has been retired for nineteen years now, but his eyes still light up when he talks about the days he spent on foot, following trails no one else could see across the ranches of the Big Bend. "It was fun," he told me. "I loved the challenge and I liked working outdoors. I wanted to be the best and I was, in this part of the world, anyway." Peiser was known in the Border Patrol not only for his ability but for his stamina and his tenacity. When his granddaughter, Tess Seipp, was in the fifth grade, she produced a biography of Peiser for a class project. One of Peiser's colleagues wrote her a letter describing Peiser's pursuit of a man who had broken into a ranch house near Casa Piedra, stolen a gun and some jewelry, and headed for Mexico. Peiser and his partner picked up the thief's trail the next morning and pursued him on foot all day, covering twenty miles of some of the roughest country in the Big Bend, before finally running him to earth about a half mile this side of the Rio Grande. Peiser's colleague wrote, "An officer of less stamina, confidence, and abilities would have given up long ago, but not Billy D. Onward he went with his usual perseverance."

Peiser told me that he had no experience as a tracker before he joined the Border Patrol in 1961, but he had always loved being outdoors. He was born in 1934 and grew up on a cotton farm on the Concho River, near the town of Veribest. He graduated from San Angelo College in the middle of the drought of the 1950s. "We had two hundred acres and we made three bales of cotton that year," he told me. "I decided that wasn't for me, so I went to work on a gravity crew." He worked on oil exploration survey parties all over the Southwest for a few years and then joined the Border Patrol in Yuma, Arizona. "The soil around Yuma was real powdery," he said, "and it was easy to see footprints." He soon discovered that he had a talent for seeing things other people could not see. "I could see footprints in a drag from a car going fifty miles an hour," he said. A drag, he explained, is the plowed strip that the Border Patrol maintains along the right-of-way of east-west roads near the border, which patrol agents examine daily, looking for indications that someone had crossed it on foot—"cutting for sign," Peiser called it.

Once Peiser had spotted the sign, it was his job to follow whoever had made it, and if they turned out to be illegal immigrants, to apprehend them. A large part of his success came from knowing the country. He was transferred to Marfa in 1964, and within a few years, he said, "I knew every road, every windmill, every fence line, every gate. If you didn't know that, you could waste a lot of time." Speed was important, he pointed out, "because whoever you're tracking is ahead of you and they are moving, too. You've got to move faster if you are going to catch them." He tried to explain to me how to tell how old footprints were. "If they've got bird tracks or bug tracks in them, they've been there a while," he said. Then he added, "Early in the morning new tracks have a different color. They're shinier." When I pressed him for a more precise definition he just said, "They're shinier, that's all. I can't explain it." I suspect he was talking about sheer instinct.

Tracking is more difficult in rocky country, Peiser said. "You keep your eyes on the ground and look for kicked rocks, broken sticks, and crushed grass. It's harder. And then when they get on the railroad tracks and step on the ties it's real hard." Peiser express-es admiration for the evasion skills of some of the men he has trailed. Once he and some other agents were following a trail made by a group that had come up over the Candelaria rim and were headed toward US 90 near Valentine. The agents lost the trail in the grassy flats near the highway, an area of tall grass and shallow gullies. They were sure the group had not crossed the highway, but night fell before they could locate them. The next morning Peiser picked up the trail on the other side of the high-way and soon had the immigrants in custody. He asked them if they had seen any border patrolmen on the flat the night before, and one of the men turned around and showed Peiser a tobacco stain on the back of his shirt. He had been lying in a gully covered with grass when Peiser had spit out a wad of his chewing tobacco.

Peiser has helped track lost hikers in the Big Bend National Park, but ninety-nine percent of his work was tracking illegal im-migrants. He says it is a lot easier to track people who know where they are going. "People who have a destination tend to move in a straight line toward some landmark, like Mount Livermore or Needle Peak, and they stop at windmills or tanks for water and leave signs. People who are lost wander around every which way."

Bill Peiser loves being alone in the wide-open spaces of the Big Bend. Shortly after I met him five years ago, I heard him say some-thing that I think is a key to his character. My wife and I had just moved here from Washington, DC, and we were still adjusting to the sparse population of far West Texas. We had spent a Saturday in Midland and were astonished that on the way home we did not pass more than a dozen cars in the seventy miles between Pecos and Fort Davis. The next day, during the coffee hour after church, I overheard Peiser telling someone that he had made the same drive at the same time that we had. "And do you know," he said, "that after we got off the interstate it was wall-to-wall traffic all the way from Pecos to Fort Davis?"

February 21, 2008

✥ 45 ✥

THE PAISANO

THE OTHER NIGHT my wife and I had dinner at one of our favorite Marfa restaurants, The Blue Javelina. We had just been seated at a table by the big plate glass window and had picked up our menus when I glanced out the window and saw a roadrunner standing on the gravel surface of the patio, not six feet away. He had a lizard clamped in his beak, his feathers were ruffled, and his bright eye was looking right at me. He seemed to be saying, "I'm about to enjoy my dinner, too." Then an approaching guest startled him and he scurried off behind the low wall, the lizard wriggling in his beak. I felt a surge of amused affection for this fellow diner.

The roadrunner is not a dignified bird. His tousled crest and cocked head give him a somewhat raffish look, reminding one of a good-natured but disreputable drinking companion. His long beak, skinny legs, big feet, and stuttering gait produce a clownish effect that makes him difficult to take as seriously as one would a peacock. He is not a lawn ornament, but he is a scrapper and probably a rounder, a morally deficient bird.

Scientifically speaking, the roadrunner is a *Geococcyx californianus*. Roadrunners prefer walking and running to flying and have been clocked at speeds up to seventeen miles per hour. They eat insects, lizards, snakes, scorpions, and small birds, and they have a lifespan of seven or eight years if they don't succumb to hawks, house cats, raccoons, snakes, or coyotes. Some authorities say that they mate for life. The females lay two to twelve eggs over a three-day period every spring. Usually only three or four chicks survive to become fully feathered.

The roadrunner is a member of the cuckoo family (*Geococcyx* is Greek for earth-cuckoo), a family with a long history of affectionate relations with humans and about which a large body of Anglo-American folklore has grown up, including the little song that goes, *The cuckoo is a pretty bird / She wobbles as she flies / She brings us good tidings / And tells us no lies*. (It was only the other day that I realized that the "wobbles" that I learned as a child probably started out as "warbles.") But there is little Anglo-American folklore about roadrunners because their range is limited to the deserts of the southwestern United States and northern Mexico, and Anglo-Americans did not encounter them until the 1840s. Their first mention in print seems to be in the Santa Fe trader Josiah Gregg's *Commerce of the Prairies*, published in 1844. Gregg calls them by their Spanish name, *paisanos*, and he tells his readers that in Chihuahua they are domesticated and kept around the house like cats to keep the premises free of mice.

Paisano is only one of several names the roadrunner goes by. He is also known as a *churea*, a chaparral cock, a Mexican peacock, a snake bird, a lizard bird, a war bird, and a Texas bird-of-paradise. The last once prompted a visitor who saw one identified by that name near Sanderson to say, "Well, he's a hell of a long way from home." Roy Bedicheck, in his *Adventures With A Texas Naturalist*, says that of all the names he prefers *paisano*, "because it is euphonious and because often in the lonely desert this lovely bird will travel along with you for miles, staying only a few yards ahead. The word *paisano* suggests congenial companionship, fraternization, fellow countryman, or fellow traveler. . . ."

The roadrunner's slightly comic aspect induced Warner Brothers animation director Chuck Jones in 1949 to create a series of forty-odd cartoon shorts in which an intrepid roadrunner consistently foils a hungry coyote. The animated roadrunner's "beep-beep," actually more of a "meep-meep," imitated by my third-grade contemporaries on school playgrounds all over the world, was the voice of Disney employee Paul Julian, who originally employed the sound to move people out of his way as he was hurrying around the studio. The real roadrunner's call sounds something like a dove, a descending series of "coos."

The roadrunner has been the official state bird of New Mexico since 1949 (how do states get state birds, anyway?), but it has also played a minor role in the heraldry of Texas. In 1932 San Antonio artist Ben Meade drew a stylized roadrunner to decorate the cover of the program for the eighteenth annual meeting of the Texas Folklore Society. At the business session, the society voted to adopt the roadrunner as its "brand, emblem, and totem." Meade's roadrunner was somewhat streamlined in an art deco style—its neck, back, and tail formed one continuous line—and a few years later Betty Boatright, whose husband Mody Boatright was then president of the Texas Folklore Society, drew another one in a more realistic position, with its tail cocked at a jaunty angle. J. Frank Dobie, who was the editor of the society's publications, liked Betty Boatright's roadrunner so much that he started using it on the title page of the society's publications and on its stationery and eventually on his own stationery; you might say he made it into his personal symbol. He became so closely identified with the eccentric bird that people from all over the world sent him carved and painted representations of it, and when he bought a small ranch outside of Austin in 1959 he named it Paisano. The name has been perpetuated in the Dobie-Paisano Fellowships, residencies at the ranch offered to writers by the Texas Insitute of Letters.

A Mexican folktale collected by Jovita Gonzales and published by Dobie in one of those volumes with the *paisano* on the flyleaf may explain my affection for roadrunners. Back when the world was young, the story goes, all of the animals were organized into tribes with kings and hierarchies of their own. The eagle was the king of the birds, and he surrounded himself with a court of nobles—the cardinals, the scissortails, and the hawks. The roadrunner was pretty far down on the social scale, but because he was related to the pheasant, he gave himself airs above his station, pushing himself where he was not wanted and addressing the nobler birds as his social equal. One day he burst unannounced into the eagle's throne room while the eagle was meeting with his council, and the eagle was so angered by his gall that he banished him from the bird family and deprived him of the power of flight, telling him that he would spend the rest of his life on the ground eating snakes and scorpions. And he has.

I guess I've always been sympathetic to outcasts.

May 29, 2008

✤ 46 ✤

RUBE EVANS AND POLO

ALTHOUGH we tend to think of polo as an Eastern sport played by millionaires with names like Harry Payne Whitney and Devereux Milburn, it was introduced into Texas in the 1890s by the army and was avidly played by cavalry officers in San Antonio and at posts across West Texas. From those posts it seeped onto neighboring ranches and was taken up by cowboys who did not always play by American Polo Association rules. When my mother was a young woman, about the time of the First World War, she was visiting an aunt and uncle on their ranch in Wise County and borrowed a horse to ride over to a neighboring ranch. Shortly after starting out, she returned to the house to report that she could not get her horse past a certain thorny bush beside the road. "Oh, you'll have to go across the pasture," her uncle told her. "That bush is one of the goals when we play polo. No horse on this ranch will go past it."

In fact, one of the greatest polo players of all time was a Texas cowboy, Cecil Smith of Boerne, who learned to play while training polo ponies for an Austin horse dealer. In 1933 Smith led a Western team to victory over the East in an East-West match at Lake Forest, Illinois, causing polo player Will Rogers to remark that "the hillbillies beat the dudes and took the polo championship of the world out of the drawing room and into the bunkhouse." Smith went on to take a US team to England and win five titles, including the King's Coronation Cup. During his career his teams won the United States Open seven times, the Pacific Coast Open seven times, and the Monty Waterbury Cup four times. Smith was rated as a ten-goal player, the highest ranking a polo player can receive.

Polo is a game that calls for expert horsemanship and a great deal of stamina on the part of both rider and horse. The play is divided into six periods called chukkers, each lasting seven and a half minutes. Players usually change horses after every chukker. The point, of course, is to move a little ball through the opposing team's goal, using long-handled mallets to hit the ball from horseback. Although polo seems to have originated several thousand years ago in Persia, modern polo derives from a game played by native royalty in India in the early nineteenth century. The British army picked it up there and brought it to England in the 1870s and '80s, and from England it spread to the United States, where it was particularly popular in cavalry regiments. Generals Patton, Pershing, and Wainwright were all accomplished polo players.

Rube Evans of Marfa is probably the Big Bend's most accomplished polo player, and certainly its most colorful. I interviewed Evans last winter in connection with a column I was writing about his father-in-law George Jones and somehow we kept getting onto the subject of polo. Evans is an affable, easygoing man in his late seventies and it is somehow difficult to picture him as the daredevil polo player that he says he was in his twenties, but he has the pictures to prove it. One in particular, which was on the front page of the sports section of the *New York Times* in 1952, shows him at the National Collegiate Polo Championship in New York's Squadron A Armory, playing for New Mexico Military Institute. He is riding hell-for-leather straight at a Princeton player, his mallet raised in his right hand, preparing to brain his opponent. He told me that he got control of himself at the last split second and let the man pass without striking a blow. "That impulse to maim," he told me, "is what Will Rogers had in mind when he said, 'They call polo the sport of gentlemen for the same reason that they call a tall guy Shorty.'"

Evans, who was born in El Paso in 1929 but whose family moved to a ranch north of Winston, New Mexico in 1934, saw his first polo match when he was nine years old. His cousin Bob Evans was captain of the New Mexico Military Institute team, and the whole family went to El Paso to watch NMMI play at Fort Bliss. Evans told me that he decided right then that he wanted to go to NMMI and he wanted to play polo. As it worked out, he did not go to school at all until he reached the seventh grade but was homeschooled at the family ranch. He entered NMMI in the tenth grade and immediately joined the polo team, playing for them for seven years. He says he graduated with a commission in the army and a PhD in polo.

Evans told me that the high point of his polo career may have come while he was still in college. A NMMI classmate from Mexico invited the entire NMMI polo team to Mexico City for a week to play a series of matches in Chapultepec Park against President Miguel Aleman's team, captained by the president's son. The NMMI players traveled to Mexico City by train with their horses in special boxcars. They arrived on a Saturday night and played their first game the next day, losing it 11 to 3. Their game improved as the players and their horses got used to the altitude, and the last game was a tie and went into overtime. They played an overtime chukker and there was still no score. Finally, toward the end of the second extra chukker, Evans saw an opening and hit the ball so hard that a piece of it chipped off as it flew through the goal. The Mexican team protested that the goal did not count because the entire ball did not go between the goal posts, but the referees ruled that two-thirds of it did and that made it a valid goal. Evans's mother was in the audience and she jumped onto the field from a seven-foot wall to congratulate him. It was his twenty-first birthday.

When Evans graduated from NMMI, he was commissioned as a second lieutenant in the army and sent to Korea, and he forgot about polo for a while, but when he was thirty-five he joined a Midland team and subsequently played all over the United States, Mexico, and England for twenty-three more years. He was part of the team that won the 1970 US Open and he once stayed in Buckingham Palace as a guest of the queen, but he says his brightest polo memory is of that Saturday afternoon in Chapultepec Park. "It was the best birthday present I ever had," he told me.

September 18, 2008

✤ 47 ✤

BEAR CAGES AND SANTAFEES

EVERAL YEARS AGO I WAS enjoying a cool Saturday afternoon beer in a Fort Worth bar when a somewhat bleary-eyed old boy on the next stool began a rambling account of his adventures the night before. "I was driving home on the Weatherford Highway," he said, "and damn if I didn't hit a bear cage right in the middle of the road and went into the ditch."

"What did you hit?" I asked.

"A bear cage," he repeated.

"What was a bear cage doing in the middle of the road?" I asked, envisioning a cage full of bears.

"Why," he said, "the highway department put it there to keep people from running into the ditch."

I love the common speech of Texas. People who can turn a barricade into a bear cage are definitely worth listening to. Not long ago I repeated this story to my friend Jim Bratcher, a retired English professor who leads the life of a semi-hermit at Bulverde, on the edge of the Hill Country. Bratcher said, "I can top that. I knew an old man up in Wise County who told me that he thought something was stealing milk out of the milk pans in his diary house. He went out there one night and found a giant santafee sucking milk out of the pan. I asked him exactly what it was and he explained it was one of those long insects with hundreds of legs, a santafee."

This is what linguists call an eggcorn, the substitution of familiar words for unfamiliar ones with similar sounds. The term comes from someone who habitually called acorns "eggcorns." The classic example is the line in the Carter Family song

"Wildwood Flower" that goes, *The myrtle so bright with emerald dew / The pale and the leader and eyes look like blue,* which makes no sense, but that is the way Mother Maybelle sang it. The person who wrote the song in 1860 actually wrote, *The myrtle so bright with emerald hue / The pale oleander with eyes of bright blue.*

But a phrase doesn't need to be an eggcorn to be a Texasism. I used to know an old rancher in South Texas whose invariable reply to the question, "How're you doin'?" was "Well, I've still got the forked end down." Unless, that is, he was engaged in obvious physical exertion, such as dancing up a storm on Saturday night, in which case his reply was, "Why, I'm sick in bed."

Sometimes it's not even a phrase, just a word. My grandmother, who was born in Texas in 1877, employed the adverb "directly," as in the sentence, "I'll do that directly," not in the usual nineteenth-century sense of "immediately," but in the peculiarly Texan sense of "when I get around to it and if you know what's good for you, don't ask me again." Another one of her special words was "plausible," which she used to describe someone who was outwardly respectable but whom she instinctively knew would be unreliable.

Some words had definite class connotations. To many Texans, a couch or a sofa was a davenport. Not to my mother. She was the daughter of parents who were the first generation of their families to get off the cotton farm and move into town—her father was a druggist—and she abhorred anything that sounded "country." Country people wore bib overalls and drank Peruna on Saturday and said "davenport" and my mother said "couch," and never the twain should meet. However, my mother could only halfway escape from the country word "rench," meaning "rinse." She rinsed the soap out of her laundry, but she renched the dishes off before washing them.

Not long ago, my wife and I got into a discussion about whether things that were diagonally across from each other were kitty-cornered or cata-cornered. To my grandmother they were catawampused. And to her, angry people threw cat fits, not hissy fits. In fact, I never heard of hissy fits until I went to college, and even today it is a word I associate with sorority girls from Dallas. By the way, to some older Texans, things that were catawampused were antigodlin to each other. But antigodlin could also mean out of plumb, as in, "that building is all antigodlin."

In my grandmother's day, human Texans sometimes got the fan-tods and Texas horses got the stampers. The fan-tods were similar to the creeps or the heebie-jeebies, as in, "that man gives me the fan-tods," but they could be serious enough to put a person, especially a female, in bed ("Aunt Pearl's in bed with the fan-tods today"). The stampers was an equine upper respiratory tract infection. I once tried to suggest to a man my age who was using this term that perhaps he meant "distemper" and he said quite emphatically, "No, there's two diseases that horses get, the staggers and the stampers. The staggers is worse than the stampers."

When old-time Texans left a place in a hurry, they said that they were lighting a shuck out of there, calling up an image of a man leaving a campfire and lighting the tip of a corn shuck from it to light his way to his bedroll in the dark. When they wanted to say that someone had lived in a place for a long time, they said he had been there since who laid the chunk. I think this comes from their familiarity with the Old Testament and with God's asking Job where he had been when God laid the cornerstone of the earth, but I am not sure about that. Who knows where the phrase "around Robin Hood's barn" (to indicate a circuitous route) comes from? Robin Hood lived in Sherwood Forest, far from any barns, but the phrase must have come from England to the South and made its way to Texas with the cotton kingdom.

Another Texas word with Elizabethan overtones is "courting." This was still in use when I was a teenager in the 1950s. By then it did not mean paying weekly calls to young ladies, it meant necking, as in, "they were courting up a storm in the back seat." But it had a wonderful old-fashioned sound, and it somehow made the activity sound more decorous. It was in the same tradition as my grandmother's referring to affectionate kisses as "Yankee dimes." And that is pure Texas.

December 11, 2008

✤ 48 ✤

TWO JUMPS AND OLD FOLKS

MY FRIEND Jim Bratcher of Bulverde and I have been carrying on an e-mail conversation about whether the West maintained its distinctive cultural characteristics through the twentieth century and into the twenty-first, or whether they were completely eroded by the mass culture of post-World War II America. I am contending that one piece of evidence of the West's continued exceptionalism can be found in the matter of nicknames. Men in the East have nicknames like Chip and Chuck and Junior. Men in the West have nicknames like Two Jumps and Old Folks.

In the East, male nicknames are bestowed by doting parents, which is probably why they are so insipid. In the West, nicknames are awarded by peer groups, and receiving one is a rite of passage. Men are judged by how they respond to their nickname. In his classic book about cowboy life, *We Pointed Them North*, Edward C. "Teddy Blue" Abbott tells how he came to be called Teddy Blue. As a very young man he was backstage in a music hall in Miles City, Montana, horsing around with one of the actresses, when he tripped and fell through a thin partition onto the stage. Finding himself in front of an audience, he grabbed a chair and started bucking it across the stage, shouting, "Whoa, Blue! Whoa, Blue!" The manager shouted, "Hey, Blue, come out of there!" The audience took it up, and, as Abbott says, "When I went out of that theatre I was Blue, and Teddy Blue I have been for fifty-five years since."

Two Jumps was a cowboy who once worked for Kerrville cartoonist Ace Reid's father. He was called Two Jumps because he could never stay on a bucking horse longer than two jumps. Long after he had left ranch employment, Reid saw his picture on television and called his father, saying that Two Jumps was now a professional safecracker and was on the FBI's Ten Most Wanted list. "Well," said Reid's father, "if he could have rode a horse he probably never would have changed professions."

Old Folks Bradford was a Texas A&M classmate of my father's, a boy from Tennessee whose movements were so slow and lackadaisical that his roommates fixed this nickname on him. According to my father's 1924 college annual, he also had classmates nicknamed Corkscrew, Blister, Sweet Talk, Churn Dasher, Hungry, Squads Right, Ten Flat, and Snow Digger. Snow Digger was from New Hampshire.

The origins of some nicknames are lost in obscurity. There was a West Texas cowboy in the 1920s called Bell Cord Rutherford. Elmer Kelton says that he heard that he was called that because as a boy he wanted a rope, so he climbed a church steeple and stole the bell cord. Other folks claimed it had to do with his impulsive yanking of the emergency bell cord on a train. Everyone in West Texas knew Bell Cord, and everyone had a different version of how he got his name.

Some last names had required nicknames. Boys whose name was Rhodes were Dusty; whose name was Waters, Muddy; whose name was Garrett, Levi, after the snuff manufacturer.

In a less sensitive age than ours, nicknames frequently referred to some physical disability. The pantheon of early Texas heroes includes Deaf Smith, after whom a West Texas county was named and who is pictured in the famous William Huddle painting of Santa Anna's surrender kneeling on the ground beside the reclining Sam Houston, cupping his ear in order to hear what is being said. There was also Three-Legged Willie Williamson, who wore a peg leg strapped to the knee of his withered right leg, and Gotch Hardeman, whose nickname probably referred to some eye defect. Hardeman was so well-known by his nickname that during the Civil War, when he was a major in the Confederate army, one of his officers received an order signed W. P. Hardeman and complained to another officer that he did not know who it was from. On being told that W. P. Hardeman was Gotch Hardeman, he said, "Then why the hell didn't he say so? Every man, woman, and child in Texas knows who old Gotch is."

Sometimes nicknames are examples of reverse English. Tall men are called Shorty, short men are Pinetop, big men are Tiny or Puny. I was so talkative as a child that my father told me that if I went to Texas A&M I would surely be known as Silent Taylor. Ivan Doig, in his novel about 1930s Montana, *English Creek*, has a character called Good Help Hebner because he was just the opposite; he could be counted on to make a mess of any job he undertook for a neighbor. I don't think Doig made this up.

Hispanic Texans have an absolute genius for nicknames that pinpoint personal quirks. My friend Candelario Saenz used to tell about the taxi driver in his hometown of San Diego, Texas who spent most days napping behind the wheel of his cab on the town's plaza. He was an old man, nearly blind, and it was considered a great joke to raise the hood of his cab while he was asleep and then wake him up and watch him drive off with the hood up. He was continually having minor wrecks, so he was called *La Piñata*, a nickname that combined his blindness and his propensity for getting smashed up. San Diego also had a resident who had very dark skin and very white hair and was known as *El Negativo*, and another who was so lazy that he sat in a chair in front of the jail all day and was called *Cojones de Oro*.

Some Western nicknames are derived from a happy combination of initials and personal characteristics. Henry W. Davis came to Wyoming in the early 1880s with a group of young bloods from Philadelphia who all planned to make a fortune in the cattle business. The terrible winter of 1886 ruined them, and all but Davis went back to Philadelphia and took jobs in their fathers' banks and brokerage houses. Davis stayed in Wyoming, got a job as a twenty-dollar-a-month cowboy, and eventually became a prosperous and well-respected rancher. He talked for the rest of his life about how hard the winter of 1886 had been on him and he became known all over Wyoming as H. W. "Hard Winter" Davis.

Now put that beside your Chips, Chucks, and Juniors.

June 25, 2009

✥ 49 ✥

HORNY TOADS

WHEN I WAS ten years old and living in Washington, DC, one of my West Texas cousins sent me a horned toad through the mail. It arrived in a perforated box, and I took it to a Cub Scout meeting, where it disappeared under the den mother's sofa, never to be recovered. I wrote my cousin and he said never mind, his mother's yard was full of them. Now they are a threatened species, so scarce in Texas that the El Paso Zoo has just acquired three of them. It is a misdemeanor to own one without a permit, punishable by a fine of $500. I don't know what they would do to you if you tried to send one through the mail.

I have always had a special affinity for horned toads, probably because I went to Texas Christian University, whose mascot is the horned frog, which is another name for horned toads. Neither name is correct, because the little animal is actually a species of lizard, *Phrynosoma cornutum.* Just to confuse things, *phrynosoma* means "toad-bodied." When I was at TCU, the director of the Fort Worth Zoo, Lawrence Curtis, who was a very literal-minded man, used to write an annual letter to Abe Martin, the TCU football coach, explaining that horned frogs were actually lizards and suggesting that the name of the TCU football team be changed to the Horned Lizards. Martin would write him back thanking him for the information, but the name of the team remained the Horned Frogs. The horned frog has been the TCU mascot since 1897, when the school was in Waco and was called AddRan Christian University. College football teams were just starting to acquire mascots in the 1890s—Princeton had the tiger, and Yale had a bulldog named Handsome Dan (UT's Bevo did not come along until 1916)—and AddRan students wanted a mascot. Someone suggested that the most common animal on the campus was the horned frog, and so they became the AddRan Horned Frogs. When the school moved to Fort Worth as Texas Christian University in 1911, they took the horned frog mascot with them.

Like other lizards (and frogs and toads), horned toads hibernate in the winter, shutting down their systems and going underground for a few months. The most famous Texas horned toad, Old Rip, managed to hibernate for thirty-one years inside the cornerstone of the Eastland County Courthouse in Eastland. When the courthouse was being built in 1897, someone remembered that it was customary to place a few mementos inside the cornerstones of public buildings. A Bible, some newspapers, and a few coins were put into a small lead box, and at the last minute the county clerk, Ernest E. Wood, tossed in Blinky, his son's pet horned toad, saying that horned toads were certainly typical of Eastland County and his son could always catch another one. The box was sealed behind the cornerstone.

By 1928 Eastland County had outgrown the old courthouse and it was being torn down to be replaced by a new one. Ernest Wood remembered Blinky, and he told Boyce House, the editor of the Eastland *Argus Tribune*, about him. House was an irrepressible publicist, and he wrote a story about the horned toad in the cornerstone that the national news services picked up. As a result, three thousand people gathered in Eastland on February 18, 1928, the day the cornerstone was to be opened up. The county judge, Ed Pritchard, officiated, and a Methodist minister, Frank Singleton, was designated as an observer to ensure that there was no hanky-panky. Sure enough, when the cornerstone was pulled out and the box opened, there was the horned toad. He was flat as a dollar and covered with dust, but when Judge Pritchard held him up by his tail for all to see, he took a deep breath and started wiggling, and the crowd roared.

Of course, there were some spoil sports that claimed that Pritchard and Singleton had conspired to palm a live horned toad off on the crowd as Blinky, but Blinky's defenders pointed out that horned toads hibernated underground in February and that it would be impossible to find one to substitute for the real Blinky. A local businessman offered a thousand dollars to anyone who could produce a horned toad in February, and none turned up. Blinky was renamed Old Rip (for Rip van Winkle, of course) and, with the assistance of Boyce House and other Eastland civic boosters, became a national celebrity.

Old Rip went on a tour of the East, and met Calvin Coolidge at the White House. He was written up in *Ripley's Believe It Or Not*. He set off a national demand for horned toads. The Dallas Advertising League sold six hundred of them at an advertising convention in Detroit. A fellow named Sid Sackett in Coleman became the only horned toad breeder in the world, selling them through the mail for a quarter a toad. Boy Scouts took them to national jamborees as trading material, and an Eastland gas station started giving them away with fill-ups. It seemed that no home was complete without one.

Meanwhile, Old Rip returned to Eastland and lived out the rest of his life on display in a sand-filled goldfish bowl placed in a department store window. After he passed away, he was embalmed, placed in a horned toad-sized coffin with a glass top donated by the National Casket Company, and exhibited in the lobby of the new courthouse, Eastland County's answer to Lenin's Tomb. He is still there.

The reason that horned toads are becoming scarce in Texas is that sixty to ninety percent of their diet is made up of harvester ants, which are themselves becoming scarce due to aggression by imported red fire ants, who prey on harvester ant queens. Ironically, the pesticides employed to kill fire ants also kill harvester ants. There seem to be a few horned toads left in the Big

Bend—I saw two huge ones the last time I toured the Chinati Foundation, and my friend Linda Lavender reports a family living in her garage in Fort Davis—so if you see one, don't take it home, but guide it toward some harvester ants.

August 6, 2009

✤ 50 ✤

THEY DIDN'T TAKE PAPER MONEY
DURING THE REVOLUTION

EDMUNDO NIETO is ninety years old, but he still goes to work every morning in the store that his father, Miguel Nieto, founded in 1913. He lets the clerks do most of the work, but he answers the telephone and greets the customers in Spanish as they come in. He has known most of them all of their lives. "We used to get most of our business from Mexico," he told me, "but since NAFTA, they can get most of what they want over there, and now our customers are local."

It was 104 degrees on the street the day that I was in Presidio, but it was cool inside the high-ceilinged old store where I was talking with Nieto. He is a small man, perfectly bald. He spoke to me with such old-fashioned formal courtesy that for a moment I thought he was speaking Spanish, but he was actually speaking impeccable English, and he punctuated his words with a beautiful smile. He told me his father built the building that we were in in 1927, and that he had started working there in 1939. Except for the years during the war, when he was in North Africa and Europe with the 933rd Field Artillery, he has been there ever since. He clearly takes his duties seriously. Whenever the telephone rang, he would wave his hand toward it and say, *"Teléfono,"* to one of the clerks, and we were interrupted several times by customers who came over to where we were sitting to exchange a few words of greeting with Nieto, always addressing him as "Don Edmundo."

The store has a beautiful pressed-tin ceiling and the walls are lined with the narrow, closely-spaced shelves that you see in country stores, designed to hold canned goods and boxes of soap and baking soda. The counters have deep drawers with big brass pulls. On one wall is a poster advertising Nocona boots, showing a group of men playing poker at a round table, and another advertising Levi jeans. Between them is a black-and-white lithograph of Buffalo Bill Cody, and next to that is a framed photograph of Nieto's father, a serious-looking man wearing a white suit and seated in an overstuffed armchair. Below the image are the words, "God Bless Our Founder." Some things have been there a long time. Nieto pointed to a brass scale on one of the counters, the kind you weigh vegetables in. "You see that scale over there?" he asked. "I was weighed in that scale." Everything in the store is not old. One part of the building is full of gleaming new refrigerators and washing machines, and I noticed a rack of new bridles, surcingles, and roping ropes. "We sell mostly appliances now," Nieto said, "and other things people need."

Nieto told me something about his family's history. "My father was born in Ojinaga, across the river," he said, "but when he was just a boy he went to work for Joe Kleinman, who had a store over here on this side. Kleinman was an Austrian Jew, and he brought a cousin over here from Austria to live with his family and teach the servants to cook Austrian food. My father ate his meals with the Kleinmans, and he said that every meal was like a banquet. They didn't have beans and tortillas.

"During the Mexican Revolution," Nieto went on, "Kleinman sold ammunition to both sides on credit, to the Federales and the Villistas. My father was the collector. He went into both camps and got the money. They always paid, because they stole cattle from the big haciendas in Mexico and drove them across the river to sell them to Texas ranchers, so they had plenty of gold."

When his father opened his own business, he and the Kleinmans remained friends, and Nieto went to Austin to go to St. Edward's University because two of the Kleinman boys had gone there. When he came home to Presidio and started working in his father's store in 1939, the Kleinman store had closed and the other store in town was Spencer's. Nieto's was the larger of the two.

"We got most of our customers from the farmers along the river, on this side and from Mexico," Nieto told me. "Some of them still came into town in wagons. Saturday was our biggest day of the week. The store was always crowded. For a while we opened on Sunday mornings, because people from Mexico liked to come then. We were a general merchandise store. We sold groceries, staples like canned goods and beans, lard in twenty-five and fifty-pound tins, sardines at ten cents a can. We carried work shirts and denims, a big variety of yard goods, bolts of cloth, shoes, hardware, harnesses, guns and ammunition, tinware, kerosene lamps and lamp chimneys, and kerosene." Most of their goods came from wholesale houses in St. Louis, Nieto said, and were shipped by train to Presidio.

The majority of their business back then was done on credit. Nieto explained that a customer would come in and make purchases, and the clerk would write down the customer's name and the items purchased on a sales slip, which came in a little book that automatically made carbon copies. The sales slips were filed in a metal rack, where they were held down by spring clips. Every night after the store closed, Nieto's father would go through them and post the amounts in a big ledger under the customer's name. Each customer had several pages devoted to their purchases. The cotton crop along the river came in in September, and the ranchers in Mexico sold their livestock in December, so in the fall and winter months the customers would come in and pay their bills, and the process of extending credit would start all over again. "Those people were all honest," Nieto said. "We never had any trouble collecting our bills." The store accepted both United States and Mexican currency, both silver and paper money. "But no Mexican paper money during the Revolution," Nieto added.

"Nowadays we get too much competition from the big chains on most things," Nieto told me, "so we have shifted our stock to appliances and ranch supplies, and we are doing well." When I left, Nieto walked me to the door, shook hands with me, and invited me to come back and bring my family. I suspect that the Miguel Nieto store will be doing well long after the big chains have gone bankrupt.

August 15, 2009

✧ 51 ✧

"TEXAS, OUR TEXAS"
AND OTHER STATE SYMBOLS

NEARLY ALL Texans know that the bluebonnet is the official Texas state flower, and that there is a hefty fine for picking bluebonnets on the highway right-of-way. Almost as many probably know that the mockingbird is the state bird, the pecan the state tree, "Friendship" the state motto, and "Texas, Our Texas" the state song. These are what we might call the Big Five among our state symbols: flower, bird, tree, motto, and song. All were sanctified by joint resolutions of the state legislature between 1901 (bluebonnets) and 1930 ("Friendship"). They have been with us a long time.

Some of the Big Five were the result of national movements. The idea that every state should have a state flower started at the 1893 Chicago World's Columbian Exposition, a world's fair which also gave us the Ferris wheel and the hootchy-kootchy dance. Getting the states to designate a flower became a project of women's clubs all over the United States. The Texas legislature, lagging behind the rest of the country as usual, did not get around to acting until 1901, when the bluebonnet got the official nod. State trees were a project of the American Forestry Association, along with Arbor Day; in 1919 the legislature named the pecan the state tree, probably motivated by Governor James Hogg's much-publicized love of pecan trees (when he died in 1906, he left instructions that a pecan tree be planted on his grave). The National Audubon Society was probably behind the state bird movement. The legislature picked the mockingbird as the state bird in 1927; that same year the legislatures of Alabama, Florida, Maine, Missouri, Oregon, and Wyoming also named state birds.

The state song, "Texas, Our Texas," came along in 1929, the result of a statewide contest to choose a state song. The music was written by William Marsh of Fort Worth and the words by Gladys Yoakum Wright, who was a cousin of my father and who was known in our family as "Gladys, Our Gladys." It is irredeemably corny (*Texas, our Texas! All hail the mighty state / Texas, our Texas! So wonderful, so great!*) and over the years several unsuccessful attempts have been made to substitute "The Eyes of Texas" for it. I myself would much prefer Governor Pappy Lee O'Daniel's "Beautiful Texas," which is equally corny but not as pretentious. The state motto is a liberal translation of the word "texas," which is a phonetic Spanish spelling of a Hasinai Indian word meaning "friends."

Now you would think that five official state symbols would be enough for anyone, and evidently most Texans felt that way until 1969, when the legislature designated a state stone, petrified palmwood; a state gem, Texas blue topaz; and a state epic poem. Since then, forty-six more official state symbols have been created, including a state insect, a state snack, a state shrub, and three state mammals (large, small, and flying).

The state stone/state gem selection process throws light on how state symbols get created. The idea came from the Texas Federation of Mineral Clubs, which was seeking a way to publicize their hobby. Mineral clubs are divided into people who collect gems and people who collect rocks, and it was evidently impossible for them to agree on a single candidate for designation, so both the blue topaz and petrified palmwood were put forward. Never mind that petrified palmwood is not technically a rock at all but a fossil, there is plenty of it in Texas and it makes handsome bolo tie slides. (When the Louisiana legislature set about designating a state fossil in 1976, there was a move for the honor to go to state senator Edgar Mouton of Lafayette, but when he declined, petrified palmwood was named.) Carried away by enthusiasm for new state symbols, the 1969 state legislature also designated a 390-page poem "The Legend of Old Stone Ranch" by John Worth Cloud of Albany, as the state epic poem.

These actions created what lawyers call a slippery slope. Five more state symbols were named in the 1970s, including a state grass, sideoats grama; and a state dish, chili. In the 1980s we got five more state symbols, including a state fish, the Guadalupe bass; a state shell, the lightning whelk; and a state maritime museum (to put them in?), the Texas Maritime Museum in Rockport. In the 1990s things got completely out of control. Eighteen state symbols were designated during that decade. The state's agricultural and horticultural interests led the pack, managing to persuade the legislators to name a state fiber (cotton), a state fruit (Texas red grapefruit), a state vegetable (sweet onion), a state plant (prickly pear), a state shrub (crape myrtle), a state pepper (jalapeño), and, in case anyone felt left out, a state native pepper, the chiltepin. The marine interests, not satisfied with having a shell, a fish, and a maritime museum, got a state ship, the USS *Texas*. The biologists did all right, too, with three state mammals (armadillo, longhorn, and Mexican flying bat), a state insect (monarch butterfly), a state reptile (Texas horned lizard), and even a state dinosaur (*Brachiosaur Sauropod, Pleurocoelus*).

The 2000s have been a culinary decade, in which we have so far been given a state bread, *pan de campo*, the camp bread of South Texas vaqueros; a state cooking implement, the cast iron Dutch oven in which *pan de campo* is made; and state snack, tortilla chips and salsa. The increasing power of Hispanic voters is reflected in these selections. A potentially nasty ethno-regional face-off was deftly avoided in 2003 by the naming of two state pastries, the *sopapilla* of South Texas and the strudel of the German Hill Country. The Central Texas Czech *kolache* is undoubtedly on a waiting list. Even the state vehicle has a culinary flavor—in 2005 the chuck wagon was so designated.

There are more state symbols, some of which are too embarrassingly puerile to be discussed here. However, the permutations of the bluebonnet are so complex and so interesting that they deserve an essay of their own.

October 29, 2009

✤ 52 ✤

TOO MANY BLUEBONNETS

SEVERAL WEEKS AGO I wrote about some of Texas's fifty-five official state symbols, and I said that the bluebonnet, our state flower, had so many permutations and that its history was so complex that it deserved an essay of its own. This is that essay.

First off, I have to correct a statement that I made in the earlier piece. My friend Joe Cole of Weatherford has pointed out that even though I wrote that "every Texan knows" that it is against the law to pick bluebonnets on the highway right-of-way, there is in fact no such law, and every spring both the Texas Department of Transportation and the Department of Public Safety put out press releases to that effect, at the same time cautioning motorists not to block traffic or damage the right-of-way. So pick all the bluebonnets that you want, but be careful while you are doing it.

The designation of the bluebonnet as our state flower by the Texas legislature in 1901 came about as a result of an action taken by the National Congress of Women, held in Chicago in 1893 as part of the World's Columbian Exposition. The congress was not a frivolous affair. The delegates included Susan B. Anthony, Elizabeth Cady Stanton, Frances E. Willard, and Julia Ward Howe, and their discussions ranged over subjects as serious as divorce reform, equal pay for equal work, philanthropy, education, and civil law. But at some point they also discussed flowers, and a resolution was passed proposing a National Garland of Flowers, with each state legislature choosing a flower to represent its state in the garland. The task of persuading the legislatures to act was given to a woman's group in each state. In Texas that job fell to the

National Society of Colonial Dames of America's Texas branch, and the ladies settled on the bluebonnet as a suitable representative flower.

The Colonial Dames took their recommendation to the 1901 legislature, and a debate ensued on the floor of the House of Representatives. Some members had their own ideas about a state flower. Philip Clement of Mills County proposed the cotton blossom, in honor of the state's major crop (he called it "the white rose of commerce"). John Nance Garner of Uvalde proposed the prickly pear, securing for himself the sobriquet Cactus Jack. Finally John Green of Cuero rose to defend the bluebonnet, and at the climactic moment of his speech, a group of ladies brought in a painting by Mode Walker of bluebonnets arranged in a vase and placed it on an easel on the House floor. According to Jean Andrews's informative little book, *The Texas Bluebonnet* (University of Texas Press, 1980), the house broke into thunderous applause and the bluebonnet won hands down.

There was just one problem. The resolution naming the bluebonnet as the state flower used the scientific nomenclature *Lupinus subcarnosus* to describe it, but there are actually five other varieties of bluebonnets that grow in Texas, of which *Lupinus texensis* is generally agreed to be the bluest. For years, whenever the legislature had nothing better to do, some pedantic legislator would raise this point. Finally, in 1971, a resolution was passed including *Lupinus texensis* "and any other variety of bluebonnet not heretofore recorded" in the designation. So Texas actually has six state flowers, including our own Big Bend bluebonnets (*Lupinus havardii*), which some years grow so tall that they look like gladiolas.

But that is by no means the end of the bluebonnet story. In 1929 the legislature adopted "Texas, Our Texas," the winner of a statewide contest, as the state song. Four years later, in 1933, Julia Booth and her piano teacher, Lora Crockett, both of Chappell

Hill, Texas, came forward with a second state song, entitled "Bluebonnets," which they asked the legislature to adopt on the grounds that "Texas, Our Texas" did not mention bluebonnets. Their song certainly does. It begins, *When the pastures are green in the springtime / And the birds are singing their sonnets / You may look at the hills and the valleys / And they're covered with lovely bluebonnets.* The ladies came to Austin with a soloist, Alice Routt, who performed the song at the state capitol, and the lawmakers tactfully passed a joint resolution proclaiming it the official state flower song of Texas. I have been unable to learn if "Bluebonnets" had been submitted to the 1929 state song contest, but the episode has a faint taste of sour grapes about it.

Now we jump ahead to 1989, when the legislature designated a handsome blue Scottish tartan designed by June Prescott McRoberts of Salado, Texas, as the official state bluebonnet tartan of Texas. McRoberts was the owner of a shop in Salado called Thistles and Bluebonnets and was a prime mover in the Texas Scottish Heritage Society, a group that since the early 1960s has sponsored an annual gathering of Texans of Scottish descent at Salado. McRoberts designed the tartan in 1983 after learning that there was a Georgia state tartan. She promoted it assiduously, arranging for it to be proclaimed the official Texas sesquicentennial tartan in 1983 and, six years later, the official state bluebonnet tartan. It incorporates the colors of the bluebonnet and presumably can be worn by any Texan regardless of clan affiliation.

Texans, however, could not be satisfied with the bluebonnet as state flower and theme of the state flower song and state tartan. There was the matter of bluebonnet trails and bluebonnet festivals. For years motorists have flocked to various Central Texas towns on April weekends to drive around on backroads and admire pastures full of bluebonnets, and civic organizations have responded by providing them with maps and organizing activities for them, hoping that they will leave a few dollars behind. There are a dozen weekend bluebonnet festivals around Texas, but only two of them are the official state bluebonnet festival. Huh? Well, there is a slight distinction between the two. In 1997, House Concurrent Resolution Number 116 made the Chappell Hill Bluebonnet Festival (Remember Chappell Hill and the state flower song ?) the state bluebonnet festival of Texas. But the same resolution made the Ennis Bluebonnet Trail, a forty-mile network of backroads a hundred and fifty miles north of Chappell Hill, the state bluebonnet trail of Texas. And then, for good measure, the resolution named Ennis the state bluebonnet city. It was a three-for-one resolution, and I sense a spirit of compromise between the representative from Washington County and the representative from Ellis County behind it.

The possibilities are not exhausted. We do not have a state bluebonnet painting, or a state bluebonnet poem, or even a state blue bonnet, which could be placed on the head of the Goddess of Liberty on top of the capitol dome on state bluebonnet day, which we do not have either—yet.

November 19, 2009

✤ 53 ✤

OUR TOWN

EVERY WEEKDAY MORNING
after breakfast my wife and I
take a two-mile walk around Fort Davis. There is no better way to
savor life in a small town than to take a slow walk through it
every day. You see the same things on each walk, but you learn to
look at them closely and think about them. Looking and thinking
is something we don't do enough of in this century. Maybe we
didn't in the last one, either.

We follow pretty much the same route every day. We leave our
house and turn left on Agave Street, passing a fenced back yard
where D. J. Pearson's friendly bloodhound, Judge, greets us with
his strangled bark. You never quite realize how big a bloodhound
is until one stands up and puts his paws on top of a fence about
eight feet from you. Going up Agave we walk toward the house of
our friend Vivian Grubb, who at ninety-one is the liveliest person
in Fort Davis. Her house was built in 1890 by her grandfather, the
Reverend William Bloys. The original wall-mounted kerosene
lamps are still in it, and there is a beautiful nickel-plated double
kerosene chandelier in the parlor. Turning right, we walk past the
Presbyterian Church, which Reverend Bloys built on the highest
point in town. Looking east from it you can see the point of Mitre
Peak, fifteen miles away. Downhill, the courthouse sits at the other
end of Front Street, the old main street of Fort Davis. At this end,
near the church, is the schoolhouse, built in 1904 and now a bed
and breakfast. In between are several adobe commercial buildings
and the stone Masonic Hall, a perfect if somewhat deteriorating
streetscape from the early 1900s.

Moving on, we dogleg though three more residential blocks, past a white Chihuahua that noisily defends its territory from the end of a driveway and a pen of goats that has recently appeared in a back yard. We come out on Highway 17 at Joe and Lanna Duncan's new grocery store, which we have watched being remodeled and, during the past few weeks, being stocked with groceries. We resist the temptation to go in and buy something (they open at 7:00 AM) and instead turn right and walk toward the courthouse.

We usually stop and visit with Ron Cox, Fort Davis's broom maker, who is always at his shop early, and whenever we do, we learn something. Recently we discussed the rising price of broom corn, which comes from Mexico and is being displaced by corn grown for ethanol. Ron is the soul of generosity and we sometimes leave his shop with a sample of a new broom that he has been experimenting with.

Our next stop is the bench in front of the Fort Davis Drug Store, which is our halfway point, where we stop to rest for a few minutes. The bench is a great place to visit with tourists, some of whom ask where the Drug Store is, which makes us realize that although everyone in town calls the building the Drug Store, there is no sign on it that says Drug Store, only one that says Old Texas Inn. The bench is also a fine place to observe passing traffic, which has been moving through town at a much slower speed since Rick McIvor was elected sheriff, although about half the drivers that go by are talking on cell phones while they are driving, which unfortunately is not yet illegal in Texas. We take delight in watching dogs go by in pickup trucks. There are two-dog trucks and three-dog trucks, but so far the champion is Frank Molinar, who occasionally drives by with six black and tan hounds and a seventh dog of unknown breed in the bed of his truck. We have concluded that some people get up in the morning and put their dogs in a truck just to give them a ride around town before breakfast, as we frequently see the same truckload of dogs go by several times.

The Drug Store bench is also a good place from which to observe the courthouse clock, which has a tendency to strike eight at twenty past eight or ten to eight but seldom at eight. There seems to be no explanation for this. Not long ago it woke me up striking twelve at three in the morning.

Turning down Court Avenue and heading toward home, we usually pass Larry Francell or James King or Joe Duncan as they are driving to work, and they frequently stop to pass the time of day. Not long ago we were standing in the street by the door of Joe Duncan's pickup, visiting with Joe, when James King drove up, stopped on the other side of Joe, and joined the conversation. In our old home in Washington, DC, this would have caused a major traffic jam, but in Fort Davis people just waved and drove around us.

Several years ago my wife and I started a list of things we saw in Fort Davis that we would never have seen in Washington. Right now the top of this list is occupied by the night a few weeks ago when Jay Jarrett's horse fell into a well in the pasture across the street from our house and the entire rescue squad showed up to pull him out. Also very high on the list is the chilly morning when we passed two women walking two leashed goats wearing sweaters down the sidewalk. It turned out that they were exercising them before taking them to the Alpine stock show and did not want them to catch colds. On another occasion we encountered Fonda Ghiardi leading her horse down the main street, on her way from her pasture at one end of town to the veterinarian's at the other end. She said the horse had to go to the vet and she needed the exercise.

Shortly after we moved here, my wife was sitting in our living room talking on the telephone to a friend in Washington when I heard Kelly Fenstermaker calling us from our front yard. "Come on in," I called through the open door.

"I can't," she called back, "I'm on horseback." Our friend heard this exchange over the telephone and said to my wife, "What kind of place have you moved to, anyway?" We frequently ask ourselves that same question and the answer is always the best of all possible places.

September 3, 2009

L ONN TAYLOR is a historian and writer who retired to Fort Davis, Texas, with his wife, Dedie, after twenty years as a historian at the Smithsonian Institution's National Museum of American History in Washington, DC. He received a BA in history and government from Texas Christian University in 1961 and did graduate work at New York University before returning to Texas to enter the museum field. He served as curator and director of the University of Texas at Austin's Winedale Historical Center from 1970 to 1977; as curator of history at the Dallas Historical Society from 1977 to 1979; and as curator and deputy director of the Museum of New Mexico in Santa Fe from 1980 to 1984. Taylor's books include *Texas Furniture: The Cabinetmakers and Their Work, 1840-1880* (with David Warren, University of Texas Press, 1975); *The American Cowboy* (with Ingrid Maar, Library of Congress, 1983); *New Mexican Furniture, 1600-1940* (with Dessa Bokides, Museum of New Mexico Press, 1987); *The Star-Spangled Banner: The Flag That Inspired the National Anthem* (Harry N. Abrams, 2000); and *The Star-Spangled Banner: The Making of an American Icon* (with Kathlenn Kendrick and Jeffrey Brodie, Smithsonian Books, 2008). He writes a weekly column about Texas called "The Rambling Boy," for the Marfa *Big Bend Sentinel.*